Female Circumcision
Among the Abagusii of Kenya

Daniel Momanyi Mokaya

Nsemia

Author: Daniel Momanyi Mokaya
Cover Design Concept: Robert Maina Kambo
Production Consultant: Matunda Nyanchama

Note to Librarians:
A Cataloguing record for this book is available from the Library and Archives Canada.

ISBN: 978-1-926906-10-2, originally published under ISBN: 9966-943-7 Paperback

First Published February 2001
Second Edition May 2012 by: Nsemia Inc. Publishers, Oakville, Ontario, Canada (www.nsemia.com)

DEDICATION

৵৽৽৽৽

*To my daughters to live and know that they should not
have undergone female circumcision had it not been
for the strong Abagusii culture that their mother and
grandmothers had undergone.*

৵৽৽৽৽

*To my sons to live knowing that female circumcision is
outdated, harmful and is against the Biblical teaching and
does not have scientific backing.*

৵৽৽৽৽

TABLE OF CONTENTS

About the Author

Daniel Momanyi Mokaya is an educator, administrator, trainer, missionary and family life counselor. Currently he is a Lecturer at Kenya Methodist University. Aside from this book, he has also written the forthcoming Ekegusii language *Enyangi y'Ebitinge* on Kisii traditional wedding.

Mr. Mokaya has worked as a teacher and administrator with Kenya Teachers Service Commission (TSC), international NGO's education coordinator. He has also been a consultant and project manager with CARE Kenya, IRRES, ADRA Somalia, and Italian NGO's of Africa 70 and INTERSOS. Other organizations include Faith Women Organization and Nigore Oborabu community-based organizations in campaigning against female genital mutilation (FGM). Presently, he is the Chief Executive Officer of WARN Kenya, NGO.

Daniel holds an MBA from Fairland University, a BA (Education) from Jersey City State College, New Jersey, USA and a Diploma in Real Estate from St. Peters College, New Jersey, USA. Mr Mokaya also received His Excellence Hon. Mwai Kibaki 2005 Head of State Commendation.

He is married to Mrs. Anne Momanyi, a teacher at Nyairicha Primary School, Nyamira, Kenya. They have three adult children, Susan, Dorcas and Job.

Acknowledgements

There will not be enough space to thank all people and parties that enabled me complete writing this book. The book took a while to be completed because mid-way I lost taste and interest to continue. My wife was instrumental to awakening my urge in completing the book. At times she read over the manuscript and made corrections, and was patient with me when I spent several hours on the computer. She gave me unreserved support to complete the writing. In a special way I sincerely thank two Somali ladies Raha Mohamed and Khadija Ali Ossoble whom I worked with in Mogadishu with SACIID, a women organisation. They inspired me a great deal; and they told me a lot that pertains to Female Genital Mutilation (FGM) and marital problems married women undergo because of the practice.

I also thank the Seventh Day Adventist Church (SDA) for giving me an opportunity to work as a Global missionary in Mogadishu, Somalia where the   initial thought of writing this book originated. This was after being exposed to the real experiences of female genital mutilation and efforts to eradicate female circumcision in Gusii. I thank Professor Japheth Maranga of Moi University Eldoret, for reading the manuscript and giving useful input.

I also benefited from the personal views against female circumcision of Father Orioki of Nyamira Catholic Parish and the District Commissioner of Nyamira, Mr. J. K. Rugut for his word against the practice.

I am grateful to Mrs. Mary Bochaberi Ochengo, spouse to Pastor Ochengo of Maranatha Church, for her unquestionable advise and clarifying detailed facts of rituals and rites performed during obware and Pastor Ezekiel Omanwa Mouko — the Youth, Children and Chaplaincy

Director of Seventh Day Adventist (SDA) Church Nyamira Conference, for his insights on the manuscript.

I must thank Mrs. Clare Omanga, the first lady Mayor of Kisii Municipality who was among the first girls to attend a national school from Gusii, for taking her time from her busy schedule to read my manuscript. She also wrote the forward for the book.

Dan Bob Osinde, John Bogonko and Kemunto arranged, typeset and did the final layout.

Pastors Richard M. Nyakego — Executive Chairman Nyamira SDA Conference, Joel Nyarangi — Stewardship Director East African Union of Seventh-day Adventists offered positive comments on eradication of female circumcision.

And lastly to the late Dr. Gikonyo Kiano former cabinet minister in the Republic of Kenya on encouraging me to write this book.

Preface

Female circumcision among the Abagusii people of Kenya in East Africa is a culture that has resisted change since the colonial era and the advent of Christian missionaries into the Kisii highlands in the early 1900s. Resistance against the change of this practice is therefore as old as the Abagusii rebellion against the white people in 1907! The practice in Gusii was deeply rooted such that not even the early Christian believers and religious leaders were above the tradition.

Condemnation of this practice has always come from "outsiders," such as national and international reproductive health technicians, global religious and women rights pressure groups, senior Government officials and politicians in most cases from other communities.

Whereas medical research has always shown the social—psychological dangers associated with the female cut, none of the researches were indigenous. The proponents of this practice may have considered these research findings as things happening elsewhere but being imposed on "us". Unfortunately the war against Female Genital Mutilation (FGM) within the Abagusii community has all along been verbal. There is no single detailed document condemning this "barbaric" practice.

The book Female Circumcision Among the Abagusii of Kenya is perhaps the first original and scholarly work but with an indigenous treatise on this delicate issue. This therefore makes it a resource material that can be consulted for further inquiry and research on the subject.

The book captures and opens discussion on a matter that is widely spoken of but whose details are little known. This research will surely be a "magnifying glass" on the dangers and evils associated with the female cut!

The usefulness of this treatise will go beyond the precincts of the Abagusii community to wherever the practice exists in our global village, to condemn and eradicate it.

In your hands, dear reader, you have handy reference material and a reliable manual on female circumcision among the Abagusii people of Kenya, East Africa. In this master piece, Daniel Momanyi, a professional teacher and social worker, has explicitly and practically explained, without mincing words, the real procedure of the actual 'Female Cut".

The author's well-illustrated arguments against this practice are clear, logical and convincing. By using the medical argument that brings out clearly the side effects of female circumcision, the researcher portrays the practice as being not only harmful but also outdated.

The strength of this research lies in the fact that the researcher, as a good teacher, explains in detail, the philosophy behind this practice in the Abagusii community before condemning it or offering a solution. He points out the mystical, social and religious implications of all that was done. Best of all he has offered a workable solution to the problem. An Alternative Rite of Passage into womanhood, circumcision "by word of mouth" as opposed to circumcision "by the cruel knife" thus graduating a girl into womanhood without necessarily involving the actual cut. In my view, once the alternative rite of passage is adapted and adhered to, this Barbaric, harmful and outdated resistant practice to change will get a dead-blow. Can't we join hands that it may be so?

Ezekiel Omanwa Mouko,
Youth Ministries Director
Nyamira Conference of the SDA
July 2001

Foreword

After reading over and over again this book Female Circumcision among the Abagusii People in Kenya, I have all reasons to write this foreword. There has not been a detailed document on Gusii female circumcision other than this one I have seen by Daniel M. Mokaya. According to Gusii culture, it was a taboo for a circumcised girl to narrate to an uncircumcised girl what happened during circumcision and related rituals, *chinyangi*, but the author has dealt in detail how the girl was prepared, circumcised, what happened during the seclusion period, graduation and final handing over to the community for additional duties and roles. The book will give Gusii women who did not undergo circumcision, among other people, an opportunity to know what happened during female circumcision. The book will also be an eye opener to all persons and parties who are out to eradicate the harmful and outdated practice. The parties will know what female circumcision was like in Gusii and the life-long negative implication on *egesagane* (uncircumcised girl), or woman within Abagusii community. The book will also be useful reference material in cultural setting and to scholars in anthropology and other fields.

The author has shown clearly what happened during circumcision, its side effects and vivid reasons why female circumcision should be eliminated and has suggested an alternative to a rite of passage into womanhood without the "cut:... After reading this book which has a clear flowing and logical facts, well-wishers are likely to support the author's view of alternative rite of passage which do not cut but prepare girls psychologically into womanhood.

The author is a former employee with International NGOs of CARE Kenya, ADRA Somalia IRRES, Italian NGOs of Africa 70 and INTERSOS, Global Missionary with SDA church and Educator and Administrator with Teachers' Service Commission.

He has articulated very well a touching women issue of female circumcision in Gusii. He is gender sensitive and a clear advocate for women and humanity issues. It is clear to me at this point that if both women and men join hands, female circumcision practice will be eradicated; the time is now and not later.

Councillor Clare Omanga
Former Mayor, Kisii Town

A word from the District Commissioner

The issue of female circumcision in its various pseudonyms, together with other rites of passage in Kenyan and African cultures, continues to attract topical commentaries in academic as well as social forums. This is because the practice is enmeshed in the cultural values of those communities that practice it. But it should be remembered that culture is not an unchanging entity. It is in a constant state of flux, picking up new qualities while discarding those that are not able to stand the light of the new day.

Female circumcision has received negative attention due to reported deaths of many young girls through bleeding. Medical practitioners also say it can lead to complications during delivery. But the most immediate concern to all is the possibility of the operation spreading HIV/AIDS as some circumcisors use the same unsterilized implements to perform the minor surgical intervention.

It is clear, therefore, this is an issue that cannot and should not be easily passed over with a few half-hearted platitudes any time the scheduled period for the practice is due.

All concerned, including agents of change such as the church, policy makers in government, community based organizations and non-governmental organizations should speak out with one voice against this practice. The book *Female Circumcision Among the Abagusii People in Kenya* provides an incisive insight to the problem, and hence is a strong rallying voice to focus efforts on ways to eradicate the practice.

J K Rugut,
District Commissioner
Nyamira, 2001

"Initiates Ready for Rite of Passage into Womanhood"

Chapter One
Introduction

It was when I was in Mogadishu, Somalia, when my inspiration of writing about female circumcision started. I swore not to stop until the practice is eradicated in Gusii.

I was working as a global Missionary with the Seventh Day Adventist (SDA) Church in Mogadishu Middle Shabelle region attached to a local Women Non-_Governmental Organisation known as SACIID, (meaning) help. Raha and Khadija were women activists fighting for women's rights and managers of the SACIID. Mrs. Raha took time to discuss with me in detail and told of the trouble and tribulations circumcised women undergo however beautiful as they may appear. The sad information of female circumcision fell on me as a big bang. As an individual she was suffering and not happy to have been circumcised. Raha and Khadija openly declared that they could not circumcise their daughters to the dismay of their clan culture. Knowledge of the side effects of female circumcision, made Raha and Khadija to refuse exposing their daughters to the life-long humiliation, dangers and abuse of girls' rights. Coming from Gusii where female circumcision is rampant and accepted, I had taken it as a normal practice that was demanded by culture and tradition without knowing diverse side effects associated with it. All my seven sisters and my daughter had undergone the initiation as did their grandmother and mother, respectively.

I learnt that many married couples had serious problems during sexual intercourse, birth and menstrual flow. Sexual intercourse was painful and uncomfortable and in some cases could only be eased with use of lubricant oil (e.g. vaseline) to ease the conjugal act. Many women were being divorced because their spouses did not fully enjoy their sex life. A friend in Adale Village Somalia, a former bank accountant during Siad Barre regime, confirmed that he had sex with sixteen women and never enjoyable and co-participatory sex life until when he met a foreign "whole woman". He later vowed not to circumcise his daughters. Hawa, his oldest daughter was sixteen and whole when we attended a wedding at Adale. Many women had unnecessary additional suffering with very bad tear which would be avoided if the women do not undergo circumcision of any form.

Girl Praying for Exclusion from the Ritual of Circumcision

Source : Kenya SDA Rural Health
Services East African Union

When I returned to Gusii, my homeland, I found that some people like Pastor Stanley Nyachieng'a Barini had been very instrumental in disseminating information on side-effects of female circumcision and had rightly branded the practice barbaric outdated and not necessary in the Seventh Day Adventist Church and in Gusii as a whole. He had gained some followers from Makairo area, near Nyamira, and some parts in Gusii but it had not taken root as such. The message was later carried and spread in part time on voluntary basis by workers of

Nyamira Adventist Medical Centre. The team included Mr. David Omare, Director of Health Services Department, Mr. Johnson Ondicho Masimba, nurse and nutritionist, Mrs. Pauline Momanyi Mogeni, Nurse.

When I joined the team I became an asset. My wide intercultural exposure, attending female genital mutilation awareness seminars, reading a lot about female circumcision in Ethiopia, Senegal, Sierra Leone, Somalia, teacher training, knowledge on Human Sexuality led to my appointment as Female Genital Mutilation (FGM) Project Coordinator. The main objective of this project was to eradicate female circumcision. With this able team, we visited many places in Nyamira district to conduct Anti- FGM, HIV/AIDS awareness, Family Life and Health workshops. With the availability of recorded video cassettes, television and generator, the workshops were well attended and a positive impact realized.

Later in December 1998 a residential two-week seminar was successfully conducted at Kebabe Girls' Secondary School attended by 441 girls who defied actual female circumcision but opted for *Alternative Rite of Passage.* During the two weeks of seclusion, the girls were trained on Home Economics, Simple Botany, model Biblical women, local renowned women, rituals and rites (*chinyangi*), Health Education, reproduction, HIV/AIDS awareness and Sexually Transmitted Diseases. (*Alternative Rite of Passage* is dealt with fully in Chapter Ten.) All female circumcision, rites and rituals (*obware)* except the actual circumcision activities were substituted by the *Alternative Rite of Passage* during the seclusion seminar. The seminar was co-funded by Rainbow New York through Ford Foundation in Nairobi, Seventh Day Adventist Church - Nyamira Conference and PATH Kenya.

Female circumcision in Gusii is an intricate phenomenon that requires to be understood well before strategies of eliminating the practice are attempted. The practice has resisted change and not easy to eradicate. The Kenya Demographic Health Survey (1998) shows that in Gusii, among women aged 15-19, circumcision is

3

universal and stands at the rate of 97%[i]. It is the highest rate of circumcision in Kenya. This is in contract to rare circumcision among the Luhyia and Luo tribes, and low with the Kukuyu and Coastal tribes of Miji Kenda and Swahili.

In this book, *Female Circumcision amongst the Abagusii People in Kenya* I am showing what happens during female circumcision and why and it was done..

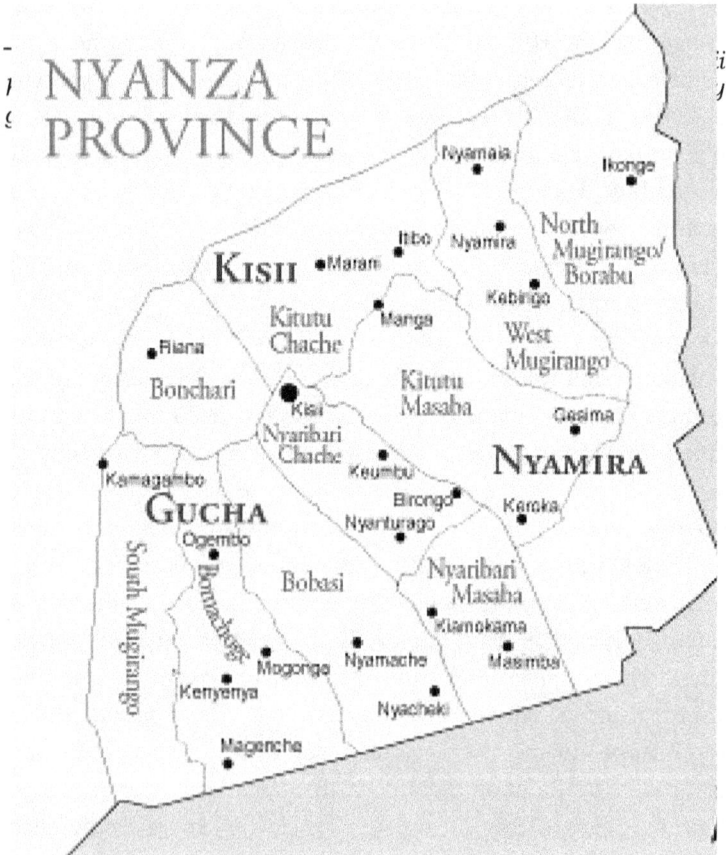

Map of Nyamira - Kenya

Map by Carlos M Nash (
http://www.uweb.ucsb.edu/~cmnash/academic)

Chapter Two
Abagusii and the Land of Gusii

At times there is a confusion or misuse of the words: *Gusii, Abagusii, Kisii* and *Ekegusii*. The correct use and reference are *Gusii* is the land, which was inaccurately referred as *Kisii Highlands. Abagusii* are the people of Gusii. *Kisii* is the administrative town which was the headquarters since the colonial days and *Ekegusii* is the language of Abagusii peoples in Kenya.

Three districts Nyamira, Gucha and Kisii have been curved out from the main Gusii land. There are ten[1] elective constituencies of: Kitutu Masaba, Kitutu Chache, Nyaribari Chache, Nyaribari Masaba, Wanjare, Bassi, Machoge, West Mugirango, North Mugirango/Borabu and South Mugirango. There are several rivers and streams which drain the area into Lake Victoria. The main rivers include Gucha with its source at Kiabonyoru hills, Sondu, Mogonga, Mogusi, Riana and Iyabe. Abagusii are farmers with a high birth rate of 3.8 % per annum as recorded in the 1998 census. With high increase in births, the land has become scarce as all Abagusii people depend on it for their livestock and agricultural farming.

The Origin of Abagusii People

In William Robert Ochieng's book - *Pre-Colonial History of The Gusii of Western Kenya,* Abagusii are believed to have originated from 'Misiri' led by Kintu. They (Abagusii peoples) migrated from 'Misiri' by moving south possibly along the river Nile and arrived in North Uganda. They continued their movement South East and arrived at the foot of Mount Elgon at the Kenya - Uganda border. Here, the group divided itself into two sections one of these groups moved and settled in areas now occupied by Meru, Embu, Kamba, Abakuria and Kikuyu,

---

1   WIth the 2010 promulgation of the new constitution, it is expected that Gusii would have 3 more constituencies.

peoples in Kenya who are said to be distant cousins to Abagusii of today. The group moved away from the foot of Mount Elgon as a result of overcrowding, epidemics and drought. Several words in the Abagusii, Abakuria, Meru and Kikuyu languages have similar meanings. These tribes are also known for circumcising both boys and girls. As Bantus, they are also good farmers and keep some livestock.

The Abagusii group continued moving and crossed the Nzoia river valley, Lake Victoria and finally arrived in Kisumu where Mogusii the leader of Abagusii tribe is believed to have died. After several centuries the Abagusii briefly settled in Kano plains before they moved to Ngoinya hills and into North Mugirango.

For some reasons their livestock died and were forced to move to Kabianga in Kericho district where they met an even worse calamity of loosing almost all of their livestock and people due to dreaded diseases. Abagusii made the last movement and settled in the now Gusii Highlands a land that produced finger millet (*obori*) and other farm products.

On arrival at Gusii Highlands, Abagusii people spread into the seven locations and 'filled the earth'. They lived within a common border which was to be protected by men, young and old alike. They were proud whenever there was lasting peace that made the old wise people to say proverbs like: 1. *Ensinyo nekona gosaka mabe na maya* (meaning the border is expected to produce bad and at times good news) (2) *Ensinyo manakobengwa 'mbamura etabwati* (meaning when people retreat and back up from the common border, it is an indication that there are no brave men for defence). Going by these proverbs, it means that Abagusii demanded to bear many able bodied men to defend the community. In the absence of organized police and military in Gusii then, men filled these demanding posts. Brave and loyal men and women in Gusiiland was a demand that could not be compromised with. This "species" was only produced and trained for this service every year during and after circumcision.

Duties and roles of women and men in Gusii were clearly defined and adhered to. Women were and are referred to as *abakungu* - (*abakungi* – safe keepers) they were expected to keep safely all that is in the home whereas men, *abasacha* (men) were gatherers, *abasachi*. Women and girls were also expected to do house work, which should be correctly referred to as all work in the home. They were to rear and bring up children, collect firewood, carry water from the river, farm in gardens to produce enough food for the family, be loyal to the husbands and their country, Gusii.

The roles and duties of women were taught during the seclusion period after circumcision. Thereafter, grandmothers and aunts did the extra teaching and training of the girls before they got married.

Men and boys on the other hand, were to defend the community in case of war, raids from the neighbouring Maasai, Kalenjin, Abakuria or Luos tribes. They also did some manual work of clearing and preparing fields for farming, built houses, sought enough grass and water for the livestock, provided more livestock to the family, made policies for the community and decided on cases in and outside the Gusii boundary. After circumcision, all men were expected to fulfill community demands without fail or choice.

Whenever the work was demanding, men or women formed small groups (*ebisangio*) and worked together to make the work lighter. The groups worked well if group members were of similar age or had been circumcised at the same time as they could have same or common experiences. The groups worked from one home to another until each member in the group had his/her turn. The group work (*ebisangio)* were applauded because they hastened work that one person would have taken longer to finish. The observers saw that many people made work easy. After working on a piece of work they were given food to eat and/or beer to drink. Since they were many they ate more which became painful to an individual who provided it. This painful offering, necessitated to have this proverb: *"bange mbaya korende 'mbariete kiane 'nkaigwa bobe"*.

Communal farming, *amasaga,* were also very common within Gusii homes and villages. Whenever a home had a backlog of garden work such as weeding, clearing the fields, fencing, or constructing a house, some local beer (*amarwa*) was brewed and when the brand was ready for consumption, a group of strong and industrious men were invited to do the work and thereafter enjoy drinking the brew. It was also common that the invited men would send a wife to do the work and later in the day he would go to join others in drinking the brew, while the woman who worked would not be allowed to join. Women were not allowed to spend many hours in beer drinking sprees. A little sip of the brew is what was encouraged for such women who desired to drink.

Drinking occasions were at times they were prompted to use a Gusii proverb, *"getiro kemogondo 'moserengeti ore eero"* (meaning it is easier to join the drinking party than the one working or doing manual labour in the fields).

Abagusii had four important phases in life, birth, circumcision, marriage and death.

Phase One of the Abagusii life of stared after birth. All births were celebrated and announced to all people in the village or community. The applauding cry or sound, *ekeiririato* of *ariri ri rii ri!* was usually announced by women after successful birth. Whenever such applauding sound was heard from a home of an expectant mother, the villagers immediately knew that a baby has been born. Short applause meant a baby girl was born and a long repeated applause meant a boy had been born. At sunrise, a day after the announcement of the arrival of a new baby, the baby's mother was escorted to east, away from the homestead carrying a small pot, *egetono.* Behind a sacred tree, the baby's mother faced the sun with a naked chest to perform a ritual to safeguard the new born baby. She humbly faced the rising sun with the small pot in her left hand uttering words as she pressed a small amount of milk into the small pot. Every time she squeezed out milk into the pot she repeated these words, *"rioba nderere nainche nkorere"* (she requested the power of the sun to bless her newly born baby while she takes a great care on the baby) after the short prayer, the woman returned home believing that her prayer had been heard.

Among the Abagusii people, sex was only permissible to married spouses. A man would marry more than one wife depending on his ability to pay dowry and the availability of land. Gusii culture and tradition did not allow sex and bringing forth of offspring with close family members and relatives and members of same village or clan.

During pregnancy, apart from physical changes, some strange happenings were noticeable among pregnant women, says Ondieki Gisairo of Borabu Division Nyamira district. Some pregnant women demanded certain foods, enjoyed from the odour of the husband, chewed red earth, became arrogant and quarrelsome, and some never wanted to see the husband at all for nine months. Mr. Ondieki further remarks that despite these problems, pregnant women were treated with courtesy and with a lot of care for the sake of the expected baby. Punishing pregnant women was rare; carrying of heavy objects was discouraged. However, light manual work and a proper diet, were encouraged. It was common to find a sister to a pregnant woman staying with her to assist in housework during pregnancy and even few months after birth. The husband, family members, villagers and even the clan usually granted requests made by pregnant women.

Phase Two of Abagusii's life cycle was circumcision. The process was complicated but all women and men were required to pass through it so as to be acceptable in Gusii. Anybody, who refused to undergo the process, was said to be offending the spirits of the ancestors and the Abagusii community. The initiation was an annual event done between August and December, which was a period after harvest. It was an occasion involving all people in the home of the initiates and the village at large. Dances, songs, feasting, exchange of gifts and beer drinking spree were the order of the day. Even mean parents of the initiates had no option other than providing enough to the community to eat and drink because of the initiates - (*"ekiomogoko nomwana ogetoire"*) the Gusii proverb so tells us. (For details of female circumcision see Chapter Four - Gusii female Rite of Passage from Childhood into Womanhood.)

The **Third Phase** of Abagusii's life cycle was marriage. This was a very active moment for many people in the family and two homes, the boy's and the girl's. A girl and boy entering marriage were expected to hail from unrelated families, village and two clans without blood relationship. The clan from where a girl was married from and a clan to where she was married to were closely connected after marriage. Dowry in form of livestock (six cows, a bull and three goats as case in Bogetutu Location) was paid for a girl and in later dates exchange of foods and locally brewed beer were common. The married woman was not expected to forget her birthplace and where she was married to - (*"tinkweba ase 'rorera na ase 'getinge"*).

During seclusion period boys and girls received training in family life, sex, reproduction, bravery, working hard and being responsible human beings in the community after circumcision. Whatever was learnt then was expected to be applied and implemented during marriage and after.

Divorce was very rare since the two families, the boy's and girl's, were closely involved in counselling couples from time to time. Marriage was sealed after the couple bore several children preferably males. Men were said to be polygamous in nature (*omosacha iroka*) and could marry more than on wife with the first one being very important. When polygamous men became terminally ill, they were moved to the first wife's house where they were nursed and buried in case of death.

Soon after marriage, the father of a newly married young man provided land, cattle, a spear and a shield. The mother in-law provided her daughter in-law with cooking utensils, grinding stone (*orogena*), basket (*egetonga*), maize meal, and water and cooking pots (*chinyongo*) to start a new kitchen and home.

A first lesson on how to start a kitchen and how to work in it (*okwareka*) was demonstrated in style by the mother in-law witnessed by aunts, cousins and other women in the family. From here a new home started and was expected to grow as an independent entity.

Phase Four: Death was the last and sorrowful phase of Abagusii's life cycle. It was a time that family members and close relatives watched helplessly over a dying dear member of the family. The family became more sorrowful than other villagers as captured in this proverb - (*bogundo mbwanyene ka eamate echana bosa igo*). Abagusii buried their dead in shallow graves, nude (naked) without rings or any metallic object on the body. A man and his wife were buried in their homestead but daughters were buried outside the homestead while grand daughters were buried even farther away from the homestead. Females born in Gusii homes were said to belong to a distant clan where they would have been married to. I believe that the reason for burying females a little further away from the homestead was that they (females) belonged to a distant clan where they were expected to have been married to.

Due to lack of cold storage and fear of evil spirits, Abagusii buried their dead a few hours after being confirmed dead. Close family members did the burial ceremony before sunset. A few energetic men dug the grave and lowered the body using a cow's hide into the grave for eternal rest. Whenever a hero or an old man died, men painted their bodies with white clay (*ebundo*) carried spears, clubs, and shields and drove cattle past the grave as they sang war songs as well as cursing death. The ceremony of driving cattle (*eburu*) which was a day after burial before family members of the deceased shaved their heads clean.

Chapter Three
Origins of Female Circumcision

Circumcision is sacred and a mystery to many of the Abagusii people including the oldest persons and the circumcisors alike. When I contacted Nyasuguta Nyakundi (a female circumcisor) of Botabori, the late Mokaya Onga'yo of Bonyaikoma aged 91 years then, Alexander Onchera, a retired teacher and administrator from Bonchari, they all had one thing in common, they did not remember how and when the female circumcision started. They were in agreement, however, that the practice was handed over by Gusii ancestors (*chisokoro*). They also agree that to be a circumcisor in Gusii, one had to be called by "the ancestral spirits". Women could be called after menopause to circumcise girls. The call was marked by strange happenings in their normal lives and the fortune tellers were to be contacted to establish the meaning; the fortune tellers revealed that such a person was required to perform circumcision in the community. Rituals and sacrifice of several goats and/or sheep was then done and later a knife was ordered from a famous blacksmith. During circumcision the trial candidate was the circumcisor's own child or a very close relative and then other initiates from the community followed.

Circumcision was done as was required by the tradition without any question. Research has not been done to establish how circumcision for boys and girls came to Abagusii but I tend to believe that it was a tradition that Abagusii carried on from "Misiri" where they originated as indicated in William Robert Ochieng's book, *A Pre-Colonial History of the Gusii of Western Kenya*. The country 'Misiri' in Kiswahili refers to the present-day Egypt and could be a corrupted word with the same meaning as that of Kiswahili language, *Misri*. The Kamba, Embu, Meru, Abakuria, Kikuyu in Kenya are said to be distant cousins of Abagusii. Linguists confirm that languages of these tribes are closely related in words with same meaning with slight changes in spelling. The same tribes practiced circumcision for both sexes but with time and change of environment, change of behaviour and attitude, female circumcision has reduced in some of these tribes especially with Kikuyu tribe.

Chapter Four
Female Circumcision Across Kenya & the World

Female circumcision known by different names as female 'cutting", female genital mutilation (FGM) is known to be practiced in Kenya, Africa and recently in some developed countries with foreign immigrants. The practice ranges from washing clitoris for the purpose of cleansing, light pricking of the clitoris, cutting small tip of the hood of the clitoris to cutting off main parts of the female genital and sewing the opening leaving a small opening for passing urine and menstruation (infibulation). One report characterizes the practice into four types[i]:

- *Type 1 or Clitoridectomy: Partial or total removal of the clitoris and/or the clitoral hood.*
- *Type 2 or excision: Partial or total removal of the clitoris and the labia minora, with or without excision of the labia majora.*
- *Type 3 or Infibulation: Narrowing of the vaginal orifice with creation of a covering seal by cutting and placing together the labia minora and/or the labia majora, with or without excision of the clitoris.*
- *Type 4 or Unclassified: All other harmful procedures to the female genitalia for nonmedical purposes, for example, pricking, piercing, incising, scraping, and cauterization.*

Abagusii people of Kenya practice Type 1 female circumcision.

Findings by Maendeleo Ya Wanawake (Kenya's Women in Development Organisation) and Programme for Appropriate Technology in Health (PATH) Kenya show that there are about 30 ethnic groups in Kenya that practice female circumcision. The age of initiates and rituals differ from one group to another. Also the Kenya Demographic Health Survey (1998) show that female circumcision among the Luhyia and Luo ethnic groups is

---

i   P. Stanley Yoder and Shane Khan, Numbers of Women Circumcised in Africa: The Production of a Total (Calverton, MD: ORC Macro, March 2008).

rare while among Abagusii women aged 15-19 is nearly universal 97%; and it is lowest among the coastal ethnic groups of Miji Kenda and Swahili ethnic groups.

Some parents know the side effects of female circumcision but still offer their daughters for circumcision anyway. That in some ethnic groups both parents consent to have their daughters circumcised while other ethnic groups as the Maa only the father has the say on the female circumcision. Circumcision is done in bushes or in people's homes by traditional birth attendants (TBAs). Many uncircumcised women do not know what happens during female circumcision. Pain and shock have been found to be common with girls under 15 years old.

It should also be understood that female circumcision is performed as a rite of passage from childhood into womanhood. It is also done to prepare women to housewifery. Because of monetary gains, some health providers have joined the trade in pretext that they are doing safe operation.

I would like to compare Abagusii's Female Circumcision practice and that of the Nandi and Kikuyu ethnic groups in Kenya- as narrated by J. S. Mbiti, in African Religions and Philosophy and Jomo Kenyatta's book, Facing Mount Kenya, tribal life of Gikuyu respectively. The Nandi and Kikuyu ethnic groups live many kilometres away from Abagusii ethnic group. They do not share boundaries nor do they fall under one Provincial administrative area but the female circumcision practices have many activities that are similar and closely related. The Luo ethnic group that are immediate and close neighbours of Abagusii did not circumcise their daughters but in the contrary initiated them into adulthood by removing six front lower teeth.

The three ethnic groups Abagusii, Nandi and Kikuyu in common had the clitoris or part of the genitals cut as an initiation of females into womanhood. The 'cutting" was the first stage of initiation and other activities were carried out before the girl was announced a graduate into adulthood. It was a mandatory process that each girl in the community had to undergo. Any woman who would refuse to be circumcised would annoy the ancestors and the community. Trainers or teachers, usually older and more experienced girls, were identified for the newly circumcised and lived with them for the purpose of training during a seclusion period. The seclusion period of the Nandi was longer than that of the Abagusii and Kikuyu.

The significance of female circumcision was to welcome females into housewifery, womanhood in readiness to handle many demands from the community- marriage and procreation, raising a family and became a full fledged member of their communities. Circumcision was meant to make the initiates tougher, brave and even more industrious. The female circumcision practice was deeply rooted in the culture of the three ethnic groups and elimination is painfully slow though with some success with the Kikuyu than within Abagusii and Nandi.

Female circumcision in Africa follows the following trends:

- Out of 50 countries in Africa, 27 of them practice female circumcision thus 54%. Countries with the prevalence of less than 50% include Uganda, Zaire, Tanzania, Senegal, Niger, Cameroon, Mauritania and Ghana.
- Countries with prevalence of 50% include Kenya, Togo, Guinea Bisau, Guinea, Central African republic and Benin.
- Countries with prevalence between 51% and 70% in ascending order, include Chad, Cote d'Ivoire, Liberia, Nigeria and Burkina Faso.
- Countries with the highest prevalence of between 71% and 98% in ascending order include: Egypt, Gambia, Mali, Sudan, Sierra Leone, Ethiopia and Eritrea, Somalia and Djibouti.

Across the world the following are trends (per report cited by Stanley Yoder and Shane Khan)

According to the same report

- *An estimated 100 million to 140 million girls and women worldwide have undergone female genital mutilation/ cutting*

17

(FGM/FC) and more than 3 million girls are at risk for cutting each year on the African continent alone.

- FGM/FC is generally performed on girls between ages 4 and 12, although it is practiced in some cultures as early as a few days after birth or as late as just prior to marriage.
- According to a 2006 WHO study, FGM/FC can be linked to increased complications in childbirth and even maternal deaths.
- FGM/FC is practiced in at least 28 countries in Africa and a few others in Asia and the Middle East.
- FGM/FC is practiced at all educational levels and in all social classes and occurs among many religious groups, although no religion mandates it.

The chart below illustrates some of these facts.

Circumcision across Africa

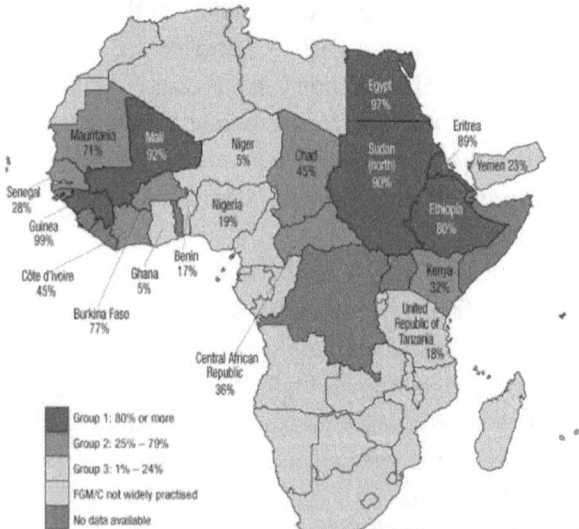

Image source: http://www.who.int/reproductive-health/fg

In some countries outside the African continent such as Australia, female circumcision practice has come with immigrants who have fled their countries of origin as a result of war, famine or political dangers.

On the African continent, Ethiopia, Egypt, Eriterea, Sudan,

Somalia and Sierra Leone are some of the countries with a very high prevalence rate of female circumcision. For the last few decades people from these countries have migrated to other countries not leaving behind the female circumcision practice. Host countries are now drafting legislation to outlaw the practice.

In the Middle Eastern countries, only Yemen is reported with some clitoridectomy. On the Indian sub-continent a small population of less than half a million practice female circumcision that is believed to have been borrowed from Egyptian Muslims. In Indonesia actual 'cutting' of the clitoris has been virtually eliminated. However remnants of the practice, namely ritual cleaning or light puncture of the clitoris continue. (Source: figures only see Bibliography No. 10 a call for Global Action).

Female Circumcision Within African Countries

Percent

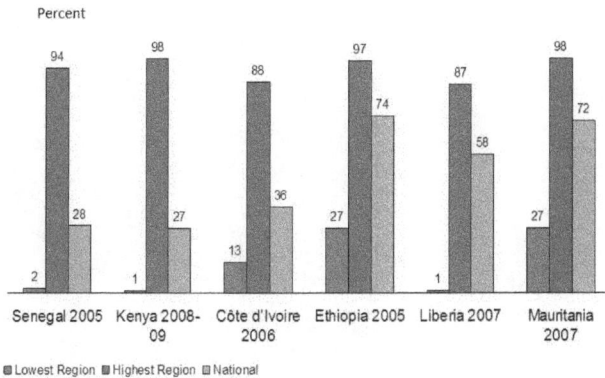

Senegal 2005 — 94, 28, 2
Kenya 2008-09 — 98, 27, 1
Côte d'Ivoire 2006 — 88, 36, 13
Ethiopia 2005 — 97, 74, 27
Liberia 2007 — 87, 58, 1
Mauritania 2007 — 98, 72, 27

▣ Lowest Region ▣ Highest Region ▣ National

Source: USAID: Female Genital Mutilation and Cutting: Telling a Story with Trends

Chapter Five

From Childhood into Womanhood (Obware)
Gusii Female Rite of Passage

Abagusii viewed female and male genitals as source of life. Circumcision was meant to unlock them and allow the continuity of life in procreation. Every woman was supposed to undergo the process before marriage. After circumcision girls got married, had sex and started procreation. Any woman who did not get circumcised or spoiled any circumcision ritual was perceived to be offending the spirits of the ancestors and Abagusii community. An offender was to be punished or got married far away and treated in a very derogatory manner; lower amounts of dowry paid for her. She would be married off to an old person, to someone with a disability, in general to a person of low community standing. It was also believed that uncircumcised women would have still births or their children would die before maturing, or would not get an admirable suitor or the clitoris could grow long and have many branches that would not allow sexual intercourse. Such beliefs were so scary that no woman would have liked to become victim. They had to undergo circumcision. Shedding of blood during circumcision is also supposedly meant to connect the circumcised to the ancestors.

Let me clarify the meaning of some common words in this chapter as follows:

- *Egesagane* — a girl or woman who is not circumcised. The word is also used to apply to a female candidate preparing to undergo circumcision and its rituals. Immediately after circumcision, she is referred to as *omware* until graduation.
- *Obware* — rite of passage from childhood into adulthood for boys and girls.

- *Omware* — (*abaare* plural) - a word referring to a circumcised girl or boy during the period, including seclusion, from actual circumcision to graduation only.
- *Ekebasane* - (*ebibasane* plural) - a yet to heal circumcised girl.
- *Omoiseke* or *enyaroka* - a circumcised girl or woman that has successfully undergone rites and rituals of female circumcision.
- *Omosegi* — (*abasegi* plural) teacher or trainer of the initiate. She/ he was an older girl/boy who had successfully undergone circumcision and its rites and rituals.
- *Omosari/omokebi* — circumcisor; in case of women it is usually a woman who had passed her menopause.

I shall use the word girl to mean a female adult who has been circumcised and undergone successfully the rite of passage into adulthood. *Egesagane* (*ebisagane* - plural) to mean a female candidate preparing to undergo circumcision and the rite of passage into adulthood — *obware*).

The rites and rituals during and after circumcision had many symbolic meanings in addition to the physical drama and impact it had to the individual initiate, family members and the community as a whole. The youths were ritually introduced to the art of communal living and it was an awakening period for education, learning and instruction.

Preparation of initiates

A rite of passage from childhood into adulthood for Abagusii boys and girls as indicated earlier is *obware.* The process included preparation of initiates, actual circumcision, seclusion period for teaching and training, final graduation and acceptance into the community as new persons with added responsibilities, duties and roles. The process is complicated with detailed activities that have different meaning and implication at every stage. There was no short cut on becoming a woman (or man for that matter), but undergoing through rites and rituals demanded by the Gusii culture and tradition.

Preparation for *obware* took several months before the harvest season each year. *Obware* activities took place between the months of August and December. The initiates aged 10 years and above were expected to be prepared emotionally, psychologically and physically for circumcision. Even though in a practical sense, most of the initiates were too young to be prepared for becoming adult women.

Female circumcision in Gusii was an annual event that was longed for by men, women, servants, relatives and friends in and outside the community. Everybody was actively involved and positively participated to make the occasion a success. Enough firewood was collected which was to be used to keep the ritual fire burning during the seclusion period of over five weeks. Particular hard wood trees known to keep fire burning long without being extinguished easily were collected. Among the best known firewood collected included *omokonge, omotamaywa, omobera, omonyenya, omoraa, omotobo, ekieyo, omosabakwa, omwobo,* and black wattle trees. Most of these indigenous trees mentioned here grew in different geographical location in Gusii depending on the kind of soil.

During preparation period, the family of the female initiate had to make available at least two houses; *esaiga* for the father of the initiate and the main house where the initiate had to live with her mother and other women relatives.

Gusii culture and tradition forbade the father and uncles of the female initiate to see or meet the initiate *(omware)* between the period of circumcision and during seclusion. The father was to live in a separate small hut *(esaiga)* into where he would invite his wife for conjugal matter or he lived with other wives. But sex was allowed after five weeks when it was believed that *omware* had partially healed.

Availability of enough meat, fresh and boiled cow's blood, milk, locally brewed beer *(amarwa)* and flour of finger millet *(obori)* cereal grains were to be available on the circumcision day and through the seclusion period. The initiates were expected to be fed well and come out fully-grown with fat cheeks and brown during graduation.

Parents of the initiate informed the villagers, relatives and friends of the good news that they are planning to circumcise their daughter and would ask for donation/s (*egetoro*) from them in the form of food stuffs or money.

Twins (*chibarongo*; singular: *ebarongo*) were special to the community since they were unique and not common. At times in remote homes one of the twins could be killed secretly in private to avoid or cast out bad omens in the home. It was believed that strange happenings could follow soon after the twins were born. Whenever the twins were born the whole community was informed and all people could not go to the gardens to plough or do hard manual labour. Sacrifices were performed to welcome the twins into the community. They were treated in very special way more especially if they were of same gender. They were kept as one person or single beings, dressed alike, shaven in the same style and treated as one person.

Abagusii community regarded the deaf, blind, dumb, and mentally retarded people as coming with bad omens to the home or family. In most cases they were hidden from the common public, circumcised secretly and most of them never got married.

Abatakerwa were also regarded as very special children. *Abatakerwa* are children born following problems by the mother. A mother may give birth to several children but they die very early or do not survive. The mother would have even up to seven or more deaths of her own born children.

In this case if she happened to become pregnant, soon after birth she would wrap the baby and take the baby to the main crossroads. The baby will be placed in a big basket and it was expected that all passers-by would bless him or her and pray for the child's survival. The baby would be given presents of all types and categories including money, foods, cloth etc. This kind of baby was given unusual names – *Nyangau* (hyena), *Makori* (wayside), *Gesure, Basweti* (python), *Onchera* for boys and N*yanchera* for girls (road or crossroads), *Kenyanya* (basket).

24

These children (*abatakerwa*) were treated in a very special way in the community. They were clean shaven, leaving some hair at the back of the head (*egesure*) and had their ear lobes pierced to make a hole onto which to hang coins and rings. During circumcision, all special children were circumcised at their homes unlike other children who could be taken to either the circumcisor's home or some other location for the operation. *Abatakerwa* were not charged circumcision fee. Special sacrifices and rituals were performed for them a day before the actual circumcision. Both boys and girls of this category were treated with courtesy and great care.

A day before *egesagane* was circumcised, many invited women came to her home. The parents of the initiate-to-be provided a reasonable amount of food and locally brewed beer (*amarwa*). After successful circumcision on the circumcision day, a lot of food was generously provided to all people who came. Female circumcisors (*omosari* – plural: *abasari; omokebi* – plural: *abakebi*) were few and mobile. They would be located first before the initiates were taken there early in the morning before sunrise.

Actual circumcision, the 'cutting'.

Circumcision was done after harvest time when most people were resting and waiting for the next season of preparing fields (*amaboba*) for sowing seeds. Actual circumcision took place after the following were fulfilled: head of the initiate was shaven clean, women and experienced girls invited to escort the initiate to the circumcision site (*orotuba*), enough food and beer to feed the community and the teacher or trainer (*omosegi*) identified by parents of *egesagane*. The circumcisor (*omosari/omokebi*) was located since they were mobile during circumcision season.

Egesagane's head was clean-shaven, a sign of serious preparation in readiness for actual circumcision. She went to close aunts, female cousins and relatives and invited them to escort her to the circumcision site (*orotuba*) and also merry with other members of the family. The invited women came to the home of the initiate-to-be a few days early for the purpose of preparing the initiate. Most of those to be initiated were young and did not know exactly what happened during the circumcision. It was stressed to her not to cry, shout, scream not attempt to hold the circumcisor's hand. The instructions on what would be done to *egesagane* during actual circumcision were usually vague and not clear to most of them, as they were not allowed to ask questions. Any initiate-to-be who would attempt to know more or clarification on the actual cutting was regarded and branded a coward and could be watched very carefully lest she spoils the occasion and brings "shame" to the family.

After circumcision, women leaders kept watch of the circumcised for bleeding all the time. Bleeding was common and many girls bled profusely even to death. In an interview with older women like Clare Omanga, we are told that initiates bled badly and became anaemic and some died from bleeding.

Excessive bleeding was believed to be caused by the initiate's mother being unfaithful to her husband. Women who had sex the previous night were discouraged from crossing in front of the circumcised since it was believed that the act would cause the circumcised to bleed.

In case of bleeding, the mother of the circumcised is blamed of not being faithful to her husband. The first step in the treatment of a bleeding girl was that the mother will surrender her waist beads to the circumcised to wear. It is also believed that this would cause bleeding to stop. But if bleeding continued the girl's thighs were tied hard with banana fibres and she was encouraged to eat cold *ugali* with sour milk or vegetables. In most cases the circumcised over bled and became anaemic and fell down in shock or died.

All females including special children were to undergo circumcision. The special children in Gusii included twins (*chibarongo*), *omotakerwa* (plural: *abatakerwa*), physically (*ekerema*; plural: *ebirema*) and mentally disabled, blind (*omouko*; plural: *emeuko*), deaf (*omotino;* plural: *emetino*) and the dumb (*rimana*; plural: *amamama*). Parents with special children invited the circumcisor to their homes since the special children could only be circumcised after special rituals that included slaughtering a goat or sheep in the child's homestead.

All the invited women, grandmother, aunts, girls and all women in general prepared their client early in the morning at the nearby bushes, woodlands, level/plain ground selected for the day of circumcision, *orotuba*. The known unfaithful women to the husbands and young women who may have had sexual intercourse with their husbands the previous night were avoided on site. It was feared that if they crossed the blood, the *abare* would bleed.

All *ebisagane* ready for circumcision walked in the cold, naked and bathed in the cold and chilly river water early in the morning before dawn so as to increase numbness which will act as anaesthesia during the cutting. The older women assembled the *ebisagane* at one area. The circumcisor in consultation with older women prepared the actual site, circumcision site.

During circumcision, *egesagane* was made to sit on the old and a non-functional stone, a low wooden stool (*orotuba*), a feeding tray for livestock turned upside down measuring two to three metres long and/or on a goat's skin.. The old unused grinding stone that was turned upside down and other seats used were believed to reduce sexual libido for girls who were only expected to be on the receiving end during intercourse. They were not supposed to enjoy sex even with their legal spouses.

The main tools for female circumcisors were: a small knife, leather bag (*esaro/ekemoya*), a goat's skin and sharpening stone (*ritierio*). The small knife (*engeso*) was made from a nail of between three and four inches or a metal of that size. The nail is flattened on a stone or another harder metal making one edge thinner to sharpen easily. The small goat skin was used to clean the sharpened knife and remove small metal powder that is produced during sharpening. The morning dew was also used to rub on the sharpening stone for faster sharpening. *Omosari* kept the same tools and used the same until her death or after she loses sight.

27

During the actual operation *egesagane* is made to sit on *orotuba* and the women force open her legs to access her genitals. Three experienced women were required. Two of them hold and open a leg each and the third one stands at the back and uses the knee to press the back. *Egesagane* was given two things to put under her tongue either *entamame rimumu* or *entobo*.

Left to Right: Chirumba (beads); Chindege (jingles); Engeso (knife for FC) and Esaro (bag to keep equipment)

The former is un-blossomed flower of a certain plant and the latter is a fruit, which is like a tomato, of a certain plant known as *omotabararia*. The circumcisor then flushed *wimbi* (finger millet) flour on the slippery clitoris so as to allow a firm grip as she cuts the hood off using the small knife. A left hand was used to grip the clitoris while the right hand with a knife snaps off the clitoris. The clitoris was cut in three intervals.

Depending on the circumcisor the procedure is either starting from the hood, and follows the left and right cuts of the clitoris or start by cutting the left, right and finishes with the top hood. Experts say that the later process was quicker but the former was slow and delaying that resulted in screaming of the *egesagane*. So the circumcisor known to be using the faster way of cutting became popular. Only one knife was used for all clients in a session time.

Frequently the small knife was sharpened using a small sharpening stone (ritierio) and the cutting continued until the last client. The same knife was used year in, year out as long as the circumcisor was in the cutting business.

Enkuuri was *egesagane* that screamed or cried during the cutting. As she cries, she brought shame to the family and was to be despised all her life by other girls and the whole village. Other girls could not associate with her in the later time. The parents of the *enkuuri* would not be respected in the community too. For this reason all *ebisagane* were thoroughly taught to endure pain and come out successfully during circumcision without screaming.

Any *egesagane* who screamed or cried during circumcision, was later exposed to a lot of mental torture and humiliation all her life in the community. All acts towards her will show despise and disregard. The following were some of the negative acts towards her:

1. She would be hit with a green vegetable called *orosaga* by the circumcisor as a cursing.
2. She would not be married as a first wife but to an old man, ugly, disabled or men of less stature in the community, and not at any time to a hero or chief's son or royal family.
3. She would not have *omosegi,* the girl used as a teacher or instructor during the time of seclusion.
4. On arrival in the homestead, site of seclusion, a sheep was to lead her to the main house where she would heal. The sheep was later killed and eaten by old women. Rituals were taught to her by old women and not the usual young girls who had successfully undergone circumcision and its rituals and rites.
5. It was believed that she would have several unsuccessful marriages. Men who were to marry her were believed to die as soon as they got married or her children would die and hence live a miserable life forever.
6. Other people in the community even those circumcised with on the same day would not respect her.

The rest of the girls who did not scream became good friends to each other in life. They visited each other and made good friendship and at times they ended up being married to one area or become best maids during each others' weddings.

Immediately after circumcision, the *abare* (singular: *omware*) were lined up in the order they were circumcised, from the first to the last. The leader of each *abare* presented a basket full of grains in *ekemunu* or *ekee* to *omosari* (the circumcisor). (*Ekemunu* is the small basket and *ekee* is the larger basket.) The amount of presents or food tokens depended on the year's harvest. If it was a bountiful harvest it was given in *ekee* and if it is poor harvest will be presented in *ekemunu*. After money was introduced the levy was either money or finger millet (*obori*).

After the leaders of each *abare* presented all the gifts, *omosari* handed them to a caretaker of her choice to be in charge of safe custody of the items.

Usually the caretaker accompanied *omosari* to all places she went for the circumcision function. After the gifts activity, each newly *omware* was given two sacred plants of *ekerundu* (plural: *ebirundu*), which were kept until graduation. The same was carried all the time she went outside the seclusion main house. After each newly circumcised had the sacred plants, *omosari* started to sing the female's circumcision song (*esimbore*). She sang a few stanzas and the group of women responded in chorus then they disperse to all directions leading to the homes of the initiates, singing along as they went. The circumcised girls maintained the title of *omware* until graduation when she will be referred to as *omoiseke* or *enyaroka*.

Esimbore was only sung in the annual event of circumcision only. It was a sacred song that announced to all persons that such girls have been circumcised and are changing their titles and add responsibilities from the community. Meanings of some words in the song are explained here below.

A soloist starts and the rest repeat after her the *esimbore* as follows:

Chorus - *EE yaye oiye....... Eyaaye oiye*
Goko okorire buya,....... Eyaaye oiye (*Goko* has done well)
Totegorere amabobaa....... Eyaaye oiye (to start New Year ploughing and tilling the fields)
Orenge mokabaisia........ Eyaaye oiye (she has been "wife" to boys - the uncircumcised - but from now on...)
Obeire mokabamura....... Eyaaye oiye (she sexually belongs to only circumcised men)

The newly-circumcised is praised with the sweet name of *goko*.
She is praised because she will now free the community to start farming activities. She will no longer have sexual affairs with uncircumcised boys but with men who have been circumcised and successfully graduated. In the actual sense no sex was allowed outside marriage.

Women escorted the newly-circumcised girls singing *esimbore* and other songs relating to sex, reproduction and procreation. This was done along the way until they approach the homes of their clients. Say if three girls came from one area, they would be escorted to their individual homes in the order they were circumcised beginning from the first to the last one in that order.

Omosegi was an older circumcised girl who will have successfully graduated in the circumcision, its rites and rituals. She should be of good reputation and a renowned teacher in circumcision rites and rituals. She would teach, coach, instruct and train the young circumcised girl to graduate as a better member of the society.

Seclusion period
Seclusion started soon after circumcision when *egesagane* changed her title to *omware*, a title that she would hold until graduation. It is the longest period during the rite of passage that lasted from five to ten weeks. The seclusion period was the time for healing, education, learning and training. The trainer

(*omosegi*) taught *omware* to be responsible, brave and tough, industrious, knowledgeable in simple botany, sexual matters, reproduction and procreation.

After actual circumcision, no man particularly her father and uncles were allowed to come near nor see her through seclusion. For example on the way home, women formed a circle around the newly circumcised (*omware*) to protect her from being seen. As the women arrived in the homestead with *omware,* the singing and dancing intensified with appreciation remarks of *Ariri - ri-ri-ri.* The women who did not have chance to escort the *egesagane* to *orotuba,* welcomed the approaching group by dancing carrying twigs and fresh green leaves, some dressed in a kind of climbing plant (*egwagwa*) and sounding the appreciation ululation of *Ariri- ri- ri- ri -ri.* The experienced women made the appreciation ululation (*ekeiririato*) longer and in a very high pitch.

The circumcised was made to sit under the shade of the grain store or nearby shade until in the afternoon when she would be led by her teacher or instructor— *omosegi -* followed by women into the main house for seclusion or hiding.

The women who escorted the girl for circumcision at this time demanded something to eat or drink (*aya erimi*). The drink served was brewed beer or porridge made of flour from the cereal grain finger millet (*obori*) or they could eat prepared ugali with special green vegetables — *chinsaga* or *rinagu* or with milk. A home that provided plenty of food was usually praised. Men were made to stay away listening to the ritual songs. Later in the day after *omware* had been led to the main house, men, women and anyone present were served with *ugali*, meat, porridge and locally brewed beer was served to adults. It was a time of great festivity, merry making, dancing and singing.

Many circumcision activities involved livestock and living area of the cattle (*bweri*). Cattle were recognized forms of wealth and prosperity.

As mentioned earlier *obware* was complicated with details for each activity was observed lest the harmony was spoiled. The main house intended for seclusion had two doors, one facing the cows *boma*, called *egesieri kia bweri* and another door facing the main gate called *egesieri kia boronge*. At *bweri*, branches of three sacred trees - *omosabakwa, omosocho* and *omobeno* - were pitched forming a kind of gap through which the women led the newly circumcised into the main house. *Omosegi* leading the circumcised girl enter through the *bweri* door into the main house. The father of the circumcised and his cousins sat at *bweri* to witness the entry of his daughter to the main house.

Omware, once in the house, was not allowed to use this entrance (*bweri*) all the time she was in seclusion; she could use the other door or a small window-like opening . It was a taboo for the circumcised to use *bweri* door while going out to ease herself until the day she graduated as a girl. If by mistake she went out by this door, a cleansing ritual would be performed involving a slaughter of a female goat.

The girl's grandmother together with her aunts started the ritual fire. The fire place was cleaned of ashes, made deeper and wider to enable more charcoal and the burning wood. In old days when alternative sources of fire (e.g. matches) were not available, fire in the main house was kindled and stayed alive. But at times burning charcoal was collected from a nearby house on a piece of broken pot, *orogio* or a burning piece of wood, *ekegenga*, to start common fire for daily cooking. The same fire was turned and regarded a ritual fire during circumcision.

As *omware* entered the main house, the ritual fire was already prepared and kept burning. The ritual fire was to be kept burning and alive throughout the seclusion. The ritual fire could be carefully used for cooking. Care was taken to see that cooking water could not pour into the ritual fire place to extinguish it or to be on the safer side, some families made two fire places in the main house, one a ritual fire and another a common fire that would not worry the family even if it was extinguished. *Omware*, her mother, *omosegi* and all women that lived in the main house took care of the ritual fire. They would wake up in turns at night to add more firewood to the fire and make sure the fire does not extinguish.

It was believed that if the fire extinguished for some reason, bad luck would befall *omware* and *omosegi* in the future. After marriage if the girl who extinguished the ritual fire delayed to give birth, a fortune teller was consulted to find out the reason. If the cause is the bad omen haunting her as a result of extinguishing the ritual fire, several sheep were slaughtered as a sacrifice to the dead ritual fire. Thereafter it was believed that the couple would have a baby. Usually as soon as the ritual fire died, a sheep was slaughtered, and blood was poured into the fireplace for cleansing and then a new ritual fire was started again.

It was advisable not to hide or keep secret the news of the extinguished ritual fire for the bad omen- would haunt them even after marriage.

Another way of making a ritual fire especially for circumcised boys was by rubbing two dry pieces of wood. This system of starting ritual fire was not applicable for circumcised girls in some parts Gusii highlands. It is worth to understand how the 'friction ritual fire' was made.

To make a ritual fire especially for circumcised boys, the following were to be provided:

- A split female dry stick of the following tree species - o*mosabakwa, omomiso, omogorogwa*
- A female dry stick called *ekerende* measuring about 30 centimetres with a small hole in the middle. Tree species of *omomiso* or *omogorogwa* produced *ekerende* of a better type.
- Small split stick measuring about 5 cm known as *enyene*
- *Esasi* made from dry leaves of *omosabakwa* plant, crushed to fine particles or dry cow dung.

The friction ritual fire was made by men only. They made sure that the stick and *esasi* were dry. They placed the female stick on the dry surface or on two small stones placed at the end of the female stick (wood). The small stick called *enyene* is inserted into an opening of the *ekerende* stick that was used for rubbing against the female stick. *Esasi* made from either dry leaves of *omosabakwa* tree or the dry cow dung was placed under but in the middle of the female stick. The *ekerende* was used to rub against the female stick. Two to three men took turns, quickly making the change as they rubbed the sticks at the top middle area of the female stick. Finally in about ten minutes if they are lucky the sparks of fire falls on the dry leaves/dry cow dung (*esasi*) and fire started. As soon as the sparks fell on the dry leaves/cow dung, a lullaby song was sung to kindle the fire. Small dry narrow sticks of firewood were added to enable the fire to grow. Then eventually the life ritual fire was transferred to the main fireplace where it would be kept burning and alive all the time the circumcised girl is in the house of seclusion or hiding. As indicated in an earlier section, the following were recommended trees that kept good charcoal that did not go off easily:

Omonyenya, omosocho, omotobo (whose ashes are also used to cure tobacco), *omobera, omosabakwa, omwobo, ekieyo*, black wattle and others.

After the ritual fire was successfully made, the circumcised girl was then led by *omosegi* in a group of women into the main house as the father of *omware* and his brothers, his age-mates and cousins witnessed the colourful occasion. The women sang the same circumcision song as they marched past the old men sitting at *bweri.* Songs on sex, reproduction and procreation formed the backdrop of dancing as the procession marched past into the main house. The story of making love, conception and birth are narrated in form of songs. Such songs were sacred and only could be sang during circumcision rituals. Unconsciously children could learn the sacred songs without knowing the meaning and implications. At a later time when they sang them, they were punished and told not to sing the songs. Obscene language used (*chinsoni*) symbolised that the circumcised girl from then will not use the words or that language for she has outgrown the childish behaviour but was then mature and was expected to be ready to be married and bring forth children in the family.

Omosegi had to have specific characteristics. She was a girl who had undergone successfully circumcision and its rituals *obware*. She was a very important person for *omware* from seclusion through graduation. She was the teacher and instructor of *omware*. Some of her duties and roles were:

- She lived with *omware* from seclusion to graduation period.
- She coached her client on every ritual during seclusion.
- She assisted and kept watch over the ritual fire and kept it alive all days during seclusion period.
- She trained *omware* to become a respectable, hard working, responsible girl in the community
- She was in charge of all rituals and rites for *omware*
- She made sure that her client was well-fed and acted a messenger for parents and *omware*.

Omware was on occasion referred to as *egesimba*. Her duties and roles during seclusion would be:

Watch over the fire and keep it alive all days she was in seclusion

She was not allowed to have normal bathing but rub her body with ashes. Only hands were washed over the *esuguta* (a type of grass found in swampy, clay soil) and before she ate.

Never use *egesieri kia bweri,* through which she passed into the main house

- Keep away from many people seeing her. It is believed that she has to hide so as to surprise all people at last to show that she has grown fat and beautiful. Fat women were regarded as beautiful and easily accepted as marriageable girls.
- She was allowed only to speak at a low voice lest people could hear her.

There were three types of rituals performed by the girls before *omware* graduated. These were *esuguta, esubo and okwaroka* or *korwa nyomba*.

On the third day after circumcision, during seclusion, girls came to see and assess the progress of *omware* and her *omosegi,* an occasion that was known as *okorarerera*. This time fermented porridge and a lot of food was prepared for them. During *okorarerera*, the girls gave additional responsibilities to *omware* and tested her responsibility, keenness, and how fast she learnt. *Okorarerera* period lasted for a day or two in preparation for *esuguta* ritual.

Esuguta and its rituals signified responsibility, care and healing of *omware*. *Omware* was to water *esuguta* daily but was not allowed to touch the genitals lest she would not heal quickly. As a result of watering, *esuguta* sprouted with new buds that were a sign that omware was healing her genital wound. She was also seen as a responsible student and was heeding instructions from her teachers.

Esuguta is a type of tall grass that grows into a small bush found in marshy and clay area. In preparation of collecting *esuguta*, a group of more than ten girls were invited and could arrive in the afternoon at *omware*'s home. Men were also invited to escort the girls to collect *esuguta*. The men escorted the girls since they would be scared to travel at night, fear of wild animals or they may be assaulted or even raped by men of another clan. The girls carried a small hoe to uproot e*suguta*. At the *esuguta* place, the men helped to uproot the plant.

The trip of going to collect *esuguta* could take the whole afternoon depending on the locality. Most of the area in Gusii is highlands and there were few marshy areas where this type of grass grew. The trip took several hours and men and girls in such trip returned home between seven and eight in the evening. The girls selected *esuguta* of a good type that was likely to sprout into many buds whenever it was planted and sprayed with water artificially. The men uprooted the *esuguta* and the journey home started. *Omosegi* had to carry *esuguta* on the head all the way home as they sang *esuguta* song. The soloist started the song and other girls answered in chorus repeatedly.

1. *Esabari nyasuguta abare- esabari nyasuguta abare. Yaya ee yaya ee, esabari nyasuguta abare*

2. *Makomoke oremire nchera igoro, tiga areme mboremo bwaborire, akwanigwe moeti na mogendi*

3. *Sese ndabu nyaeta mache ng'umbu, yarabirie ekimincha n'okogoro*

As the men and girls approach the homestead, the men took a different direction leaving girls proceed to *bweri* (cattle living area). *Omosegi* still carried *esuguta* on her head as the group of other girls sang *esuguta* song. The girls brought the *esuguta* home and placed it at *bweri* on the same place where the father sat to witness his daughter being escorted into the main house the first day of circumcision. Late in the night, *esuguta* was brought into the main house where it was planted after playing e*ng'iti* game. *Esuguta* would be watered daily by *omware*. The same night girls played *eng'iti,* a kind of instrument that is made to make sound when a stick is rubbed on the wet skin.

Eng'iti was a game played by the trainers as one of the rituals in training bravery, toughness with a message 'always do not believe' until you see by your own eyes.

To prepare *eng'iti* the following were provided:
- A medium-sized pot half filled with water
- A soaked soft skin of radius 60cm
- A rope
- A stick of about 60 cm
- Water

In preparation of *eng'iti* game a hole was dug enough to bury the pot up to the neck. The soaked skin is tied tightly to cover the mouth of the pot, with the hairy side of the skin in and the smooth side out.

The bark of the small stick is removed and it remains plain to allow friction.

The top of the pot resembled a drum top, but wet as a soaked skin was used instead. The tight soaked skin helps to produce sound when friction was applied on it. A person stands in front of the tied pot holding a stick while pressing and rubbing it up and down on the wet skin. One person held the stick firmly while moving the hands up and down while another person pours water on the hands as they are rubbed and moved up and down. As rubbing continues, vibrations occur producing a deep sound as the hands are moved up down while gripping *ekerende*. Men made and tried *eng'iti* before it was handed over to the girls.

Prior to the *eng'iti* preparation, *omware* would be told mysterious stories about it. She was told that *eng'iti* was a huge animal that swallowed *omware* alive and she would stay in the stomach eating part of the stomach for a few days. As the *eng'iti* was played and produced the deep scary sound, *omware* would be scared stiff in fear of being swallowed by this strange monster. The girls added to *omware*'s scare as they pretended that there was a strange wild animal that has come to swallow her and keep her for some days.

The game was to teach *omware* to be brave and should not believe in things that she has not seen by her own eyes. After *eng'iti* has been played for a while, *omware* was then allowed to see it. She would find that it was only a pot and common items of a stick and water. It can be very scaring for someone in darkness on hearing *eng'iti* for the first time.

This ritual is done while all the girls are nude naked. Some girls torch the grass and pass it over their heads. The grass produce some dim light and this makes the game more scary and frightening. Before *omware* graduated, *engi'ti* game was played twice: during *esuguta* rituals and *okwaroka/gosoka korwa nyomba* which is the final day before graduation.

After playing the *eng'iti* game, the pot is removed leaving an empty hole. Then the girls dress in leaves of a climbing plant, *egwagwa*, as they go to collect *esuguta* from *bweri*. After the pot has been removed, *esuguta* is planted in the place. *Omware* would water the *esuguta* all the time before she ate any meal. She washed her hands over the *esuguta* as she sang a short chorus of *esuguta* song. *Omosegi* at times would assist omware to wash hands over the e*suguta* as the *esuguta* song is sang.

Omware was regarded responsible and expected to be healed quickly when *esuguta* started sprouting and adding new buds.

The following day after *esuguta* ritual, *omosegi* and the grandmother went out into the woods to collect *amabuko* - a special type of plant with sweet smell. *Amabuko* plants were used for two main purposes: to make a small cage like structure *(riburu)* and branches made a sleeping bed. Riburu became a special hiding place for *omware*. She slept in *riburu* and at times ate there whenever strangers came into the main house.

After the second ceremony of *esuguta*, girls left *omware* and *omosegi* to carry out other assigned duties before they came back as a group during *esubo* ceremony. The ritual fire was to be kept burning and alive, *esuguta* had to be watered daily, *omware* was to be well-fed and taken care. Medicine or oil was applied on the clitoris so as to heal quickly. She was not allowed to be seen by men or else she would lose weight or slowed down healing.

It should be remembered that many girls could be circumcised at one place in a given day. Each girl was escorted to her individual home after circumcision. After *esuguta* ritual, a period of about four to five weeks, most of them would have partially healed and were allowed to go out into the woods a few hours during the day. In the woods they were to meet with others (*abare*) to share experiences. During the first meeting day each one wanted to be the first to see the other one. Whoever saw the other first became the winner of *ogokonga* game.

The second ritual to be performed was *esubo*. Here girls came during the day to the home of the circumcised girl in preparation for the ritual. They were served with plenty of food and were supposed to be made happy if they have to be efficient in the ritual. At midday, the girls disappear into the deep forest to collect several plants that will be used in the ritual. At night the girls undressed and started testing *omware* on how many plants she knew. The girl names the plants and their uses. She would be asked to group the plants into two groups, poisonous and medicinal or safe plants. If *omware* did not know most of the plants, *omosegi* (her teacher and trainer) would assist her and later by the experienced girls.

In the moonlight the girls sang, danced and played games

with each other. The songs were sex related and they touched on sexual acts of mating, pregnancy, intercourse reproduction and procreation.

They also praised their femininity and virginity. They sang on how good sexual intercourse was and how men long and love to get it. The girls sounded attractive and luring sexually. Since sex was not permitted before marriage, the men could be aroused by the songs and come around the home.

They also made plans with other girls or married women to open for them as they look for sleeping girls for sexual intercourse. At times these men managed to have sex with the girls in darkness or girls hurt some men as they try to enter the house. The act of quietly seeking sex in darkness with any girl was known as *ogochobera/ogochoba*. It was popular with unmarried men.

Graduation

Finally came the graduation ritual. This was known as *ogosoka korwa nyomba or okwaroka.* This ritual involved a few girls, *omware*, family members, parents, home people or very close relatives. The graduation ritual took two to five days. During this occasion, *eng'iti* game was played for the last time. It was played longer than *esuguta* time with greater participation from the candidate (*omware*). She acquired more skills on how to play it, its significance and how it was prepared. Graduation period was time for blessings and exchange of gifts. It was the time of burying the past and entering a new status in the Gusii community.

On the graduation day, men were invited to prepare *eng'iti* in the evening. *Esuguta* was uprooted and in the same hole from where *esuguta* was uprooted, *eng'iti* was inserted and played for the last time. It is made ready and played before *omware* was taken to the river to bathe. This time *omware* learnt keenly how *eng'iti* was prepared and played. As *eng'iti* game was being played, the mother of *omware* joined her husband in the smaller hut (*esaiga*) and waited to bless their daughter and her *omosegi* (teacher, mentor, coach and trainer).

41

In the middle of the night, after playing *eng'iti* game, *omware* and *omosegi* went to the parents for special blessings known as *okoborania chiombe na abaana*. *Borania*, are blessings in dialogue. *Omware* asks the parents in turn to bless her and the parents respond positively in turns to bless their daughter with children and wealth. *Omware*'s parents, mother and father, in the middle of the night listen to *omware* and *omosegi* ask outside their bedroom: *tata borania*. The father then replies: *ee mwana borania chiombe na abana*.

Omosegi who accompanies *omware* also asks to be blessed with children and wealth from *omware*'s parents. The blessings are verbal and the request is granted and she is blessed. The exit was the door into which she entered the main house that was not in use during the seclusion period.

Then the same question was presented to the mother: *baba borania*. Then the mother replied: *ee mwana borania chiombe na abana*. In this process, both *omware* and *omosegi* in turn ask for the blessings from the parents of *omware*. As the parents reply and bless them, they (parents) are expected to perform sexual intercourse or an act with genitals as the husband lies between the thighs of his wife. *Omware* and *omosegi* are finally blessed with children and wealth.

On the graduation night there was no sleep but activities went in order from the first to the last and eventually graduation. After blessings, *omware* and *omosegi* were to stay outside the main house and later proceed to the river to bathe.

As soon as *omware* leaves the main house for blessings and bathing, the grandmother takes out *amabuko*, *esuguta*, and *eng'iti* and makes fire outside the main house, *bweri*. From then on, *omware* did not hide but was free to be seen by all people including her father and uncles. After the blessings, a few invited men prepared to escort *omware* to bathe in the river.

Eyarogoro was a period of final shedding of childhood, wearing womanhood and changing the title from *egesagane* to a more respectable and honourable title and status of *omoiseke*. The process was done by bathing *omware* and announcing the title and status in songs.

Eyarogoro was a song sang as *omware* was led to the river to bathe and shed away the old and then wear a new status. The song explains how sweet the early morning sleep is and further states that they have forfeited the sleep to do a very remarkable job of leading *omware* into graduation. *Omware*'s body was painted with white clay like earth (*ebundo*). The painting and bathing marked the last ceremony of seclusion. After a few additional rituals *omware* was announced a graduate into womanhood. *Eyarogoro* song was sung with melodious high tones of soprano and altos. One of the experienced girls led in the singing as others answered in chorus- Leader: *Eyarogoroo* y*arogoroo, rogoro ndonga bogondereria*......... Others repeat after her.

At the river, *omosegi* assisted omware to bathe while being protected and hidden by other girls. Usually the bathing and cleansing took hours. After the washing, the girls sang *eyarogoro* song as they walked back home.

In the afternoon, *omware* dressed in new clothes and decorated in beads of assorted colours. On her fore head *omware* wore e*getinti* (a hair band made of leather and assorted beads) as a certificate of graduation. It would be worn in the last day of graduation until three days, as she spent a night with her teacher and visited a public place preferably a market. It was removed by the mother and kept safely on the third day when she returned home.

Omware then changed her title to *omoiseke* or *enyaroka*, meaning a successfully graduated girl. Food was then served to the people who came to witness the graduation. In late afternoon the father of the girl gets milk and the locally brewed beer in turns. The mother presented sour milk in the gourd or *egesanda* using both hand in full respect. The father sips the milk and spits on the face of the newly graduated girl. Then he gives her the milk in the same container to sip and swallow. Then the mother of the girl presents the local brew in *ekemunu* and sips and spits it on the face but she does not give the girl beer to sip.

The mother repeated the blessing activity that the husband

had done. As the father and mother sips and spit the milk and beer and spit on the face of the girl, the parents of the girl utter blessing word to their daughter_ *nakoa egwasi ngombe na banto* (I bless you with children, wealth and livestock). Parents bless their daughter with children and wealth; the wealth which included livestock.

Later in the afternoon the grandmother burned *amabuko* as the girl nears to graduate of the circumcision rites and rite of passage rituals. The burning of *amabuko* symbolized shedding away childhood completely and never return to it again.

The mother of *omware* gives flour to *omosegi* in a small basket *ekemunu* that she carries proudly on her head to her home. Grass (*emurwa*) was pitched on top the flour in *ekemunu* and is carried on the head of omosegi as she leads her graduate to her home or a respectable relative either of the two, *omware* or *omosegi*. The grass, *emurwa* was a good sign of fertility and having several children.

This is a very exciting moment for both *omware* and *omosegi* for successfully keeping the ritual fire alive and other rituals. The respect between the *omosegi* and the girl was immense and life-long. The following day she (*omware)* is accompanied with her trainer and mentor to a market or a public gathering place then the last day she returns to her parents and then removes *egetinti* and she was then declared a successful graduate into womanhood (*omoiseke/enyaroka*).

The significance of initiation and circumcision is that after the seclusion period graduates deemed to be reborn and returned to the community as new persons with new personalities, responsibilities and obligations to themselves, families and community. They acquired new status. For example that it was a taboo for a father to beat a circumcised daughter, or physically punish her.

At this stage the graduates are deemed to have lost childhood and become young adults ready for sexual life, marriage and family life. They can plant their biological seed so that the next generation can arrive and continue.

A point to Note:

The author has clearly documented the rites and rituals in the way they were carried out and the implications as perceived by those concerned, parents of the initiates, omware *and the community. He does not approve of them nor does he recommend the same to continue being practiced. Elsewhere in the book he has clearly suggested the alternatives on the same.*

Mr. Nelson King'oina Nyang'era from Kabosi Nyaribari, a retired magistrate, and an expert in Gusii Customary Law and author of a book, "The Making of a Man and Woman under Abagusii Customary Laws", *read the manuscript with interest and said that this work was widely researched and documented in detail than any earlier documentation. He further said that the book would be future reference material written by an indigenous (Omogusii) educator and social worker in the effort of eradicating harmful and outdated traditional practices. He further said that culture is within the people and practiced by them voluntarily or involuntarily and any change in cultural practice in Gusii should start from within by the same people or else it will be thought as the change is imposed on them. Diplomacy, awareness and frankness are crucial in influencing cultural change as opposed to force, threats and harassment by any authority. When custom, tradition or culture is not in use, it dies a natural death.*

Chapter Six
Side Effects of Female Circumcision

We have seen what was happened to girls during and after circumcision among Abagusii people in Kenya. This is to the benefit of all persons involved in eradicating female circumcision in Gusiiland. The text would also benefit women from Gusii land who because of some reasons opted NOT to undergo circumcision to know what circumcised girls underwent.

It would also benefit those joining Abagusii in marriage to make informed decisions on what to do to their daughters bearing in mind that the practice is a violation of child rights.

Female circumcision should be regarded as violence against and abuse of girls who are at the age when they are not able to make decisions on their own. Girls under 12 years who undergo female circumcision are vulnerable and are not able to say 'No' by themselves. It could be no problem if women over 18 years demand circumcision and its rites and rituals.

Dr. Benard Mageto Ateka, MB, ChB, from Nairobi University hails from Gusii where female circumcision is rampant and where the community is resistant to change. He admits that all his sisters underwent circumcision although his parents are staunch SDA Christians. He says that there is a strong force between culture and Christianity. The parents seem to have been torn apart on whether to circumcise girls as required by Gusii culture and tradition or not to circumcise them since there is no Biblical backing for female circumcision. His mother could not stop circumcising her daughters as she claims that since she had done it to the elder daughter, all daughters were to undergo female circumcision. She says she did not want to have two groups of daughters, the circumcised and uncircumcised.

When I asked Dr. Ateka what he thinks about female circumcision practice, he said without hesitation that it should not be done and should be eliminated. He gave three reasons;

there is no Biblical backing for female circumcision, from medical point of view and legal. He said that God gave clear instruction that only men should be circumcised by removal of fore skin. Abraham and men in his household and men in generations to come were to undergo circumcision. May be God did not allow women to be circumcised because of the anatomy and physiology of their bodies.

He further warns that it is illegal to cause bodily harm to a person, Penal Code Article 74 (1) states that: *"No person shall be subject to torture or to inhuman or degrading, punishment or treatment".* Further Code # 231 States that *"any person who with intent to maim, disfigure or disable any person or do grievous bodily harm to any other person .... Is guilty of a felony (crime) and is liable to imprisonment for life with or without corporal punishment".*

Dr. Ateka has two daughters who are past the age of circumcision and will not practice. On medical grounds he said that he could not exhaust reasons against female circumcision but gave a few reasons relevant ones to female circumcision done in Gusii.

He gave the side effects listed below of female circumcision. He cited incidents he had handled in his clinic at Kebirigo where the surrounding community has 100% of females circumcised.

Some of the noticeable problems encountered during and after circumcision included excessive bleeding, extreme pain, urine retention, keloids growth, painful sexual intercourse, stress, shock and infection.

a) Bleeding - amputation of the clitoris involves cutting across the clitoral artery, which supplies blood to the erectile, spongy tissue of the clitoris and its surroundings. This artery has a strong flow and high pressure. To stop bleeding, the artery must be packed tightly or tied with a suture, either of which may slip and lead to haemorrhage. Haemorrhage may also occur after the first week as a result of sloughing of the clot over the artery, usually because of infection. Protracted bleeding commonly leads to anaemia that may, in turn, affect the growth of the child. Excessive and severe bleeding is likely to cause anaemia, haemorrhage and hence death may occur.

Bleeding incidents - in December 1999 alone, several circumcised girls were attended in his Kebirigo hospital on bleeding, shock and stress. Two of them, 12 and 8 year olds, from Kabati and Nyagaachi villages, bled profusely that necessitated suturing the cut clitoris artery and finally admitting them for observation. They were discharged after a day. Several other bleeding girls were attended and allowed to go home.

The bleeding situation embarrassed the family members especially men who became anxious and worried about what may become of the girls. It is a taboo for men to see a circumcised girl and worse still it was more embarrassing for men to be practically involved in stopping bleeding from a girl's genital. A mother of one of the admitted girls said that bleeding was normal after circumcision and during her time the bleeding girls were given milk, crumbs, and cold foods to stop bleeding. For one of the bleeding girls, who was now in primary four, did not know the difference as she thought that the situation she was in was what circumcision entailed. She trusted that her mother would take care of her.

b) Extreme pain incurred may cause shock and a life-long trauma. The majority of operations are done without anaesthesia. Even when local anaesthesia is used, pain in the highly sensitive area of the clitoris returns within two to three hours of the operation. Although general anaesthesia is rarely used, it poses a considerable risk for children in countries with few specialized anaesthetists. Local anaesthesia in itself often becomes another form of torture. The clitoris is a highly vascular organ with a dense concentration of nerve endings. To anesthetise the area completely, multiple, painful insertions of the needle are required. The anaesthetic used also produces a stinging sensation which can be painful. Many doctors or midwives who perform female circumcision prick the clitoris with just a few drops of anaesthesia, more to satisfy the relatives- and claim a higher fee - than to relieve the child's pain.

c) Urine retention - Pain, swelling and inflammation of the front of the vulva usually result in an inability to pass urine for hours or days. Urine retention increases pain and leads to excessive discomfort and pain, and harmful which may lead to urinary tract infections later on.

d) Keloids are scars that refuse to stretch making childbirth difficult and can cause severe tearing of the vagina. If tearing of vagina occurs, permanent damage may be done to the urethra or anus and the girl may not be able to control urine or faeces. Keloid formations are unsightly and difficult to manage.

e) *Painful Sex:* Sexual intercourse may be painful and sometimes unnecessary bleeding may occur during penetration.

f) Stress and shock - the pain, fear, and stress of screaming may cause the child to faint or enter a state of shock. Such traumatic shock can very occasionally cause death.

g) Infection - infection can caused by unsterile cutting instruments or may occur within a few days as the area becomes soaked in urine and contaminated by faeces. Infection is very common. The degree of infection varies widely from a superficial film of pus, to an ulcerating wound, to a general toxic infection (septicaemia) if the bacterium reaches the blood stream. If not treated promptly with strong antibiotics, septicaemia often leads to death. Unsterilized equipment can lead top tetanus infection, which is also usually fatal. There is no evidence that female circumcision is a major contributor to the spread of HIV infection, although it is reported that group circumcision using the same unclean cutting instruments is still common. Repeat cutting and stitching and possibility of anal intercourse also increase the risk of AIDS.

h) Standard of Circumcision — both paramedics and traditional circumcisors do not have a standard of circumcision. In this reason excessive scarring may result. Since there is no standard in circumcision, excision or clitoridectomy occurs. Excision involves the removal of the clitoris and part of the inner vaginal lips, labia minora. Clitoridectomy involves the removal of the clitoral head and sometimes along with part or the entire clitoris.

Chapter Seven
Different views on Female Circumcision

People have different views concerning female circumcision. Most men from Gusii do not see why the practice should be eradicated but those who have attended seminars on anti-female circumcision agree that female circumcision is outdated and not necessary. The latter are a minority that does not share the same with most men. Some men know the side effects but offer their daughters for circumcision anyway. Whoever that has had his daughters circumcised before he knew the side effects of circumcision have hard time to advocate for elimination of female circumcision. It becomes hard to convince other men not to circumcise their daughters when their daughters are already circumcised.

Raha Mohamed and Khadija Ossoble Ali - Mogadishu Somalia
Raha and Khadija are Somali women who are directors of a women local non-governmental organisation in Mogadishu Somalia; they are the women who inspired me to write this book in defying the outdated practice of female circumcision. They enlightened me in detail what happened during circumcision and the immediate and long term problems that follow. They also narrated the marital sexual problems married women are faced with and hence hate to have been circumcised in accordance with Somali culture. They refused openly to Somali community that their daughters would never undergo circumcision even if the Somali culture demanded. They are not in favour of any form of female circumcision for there is no lesser evil.

Mary Bochaberi Ochengo, Pastor's wife.
Mary Bochaberi is a wife to Pastor Ochengo of Maranatha Church in Nyamira Township. She hails from Obwari in North Mugirango location Nyamira district. During her youth she was

actively involved in teaching and training newly circumcised girls in her locality. She is very knowledgeable on the rites and rituals performed during actual circumcision and seclusion period. At her later life she was converted to Christianity and has attended seminars on anti female circumcision.

She regrets the time and effort she spent on female circumcision and appeals to all women in Gusii not to expose their daughters in the female circumcision practice. She remembers of bleeding, ugly scars caused during circumcision and advocates for total elimination of the practice.

Nyasuguta Nyakundi—female circumciser

A resident of Botabori, Nyatieno Sub-Location, has been a circumciser for a long time. She hails from Kegogi and married to Nyakundi Nyaiyombe of Botabori Mwakiage village, Nyamira District. She circumcised most of her grand daughters and girls from the neighbourhood. She is in the lineage of circumcisers and after her menopause ancestral spirits called her to the art. She had peculiar sicknesses that could not even be treated by modern medicine. Having these problems she contacted a fortune teller and was advised to prepare for circumcision. After this message, she sacrificed an old goat, fed the community and a blacksmith made a knife for her and went to Riakworo ten kilometres away to collect a sacred stone on which initiates sat when being circumcised. The first client was her brother's daughter. She claims to have been a careful and good circumciser for not many girls ever screamed. (As indicated elsewhere, a girl who cried or screamed during circumcision was known as *enkuuri*.) She charged between her clients between 2 - 5 shillings.

When I interviewed her on 25th December 2000, she showed me the sacred stone she had collected from Riakworo; she maintains that girls should be circumcised. She wished to hand over the art to one of her daughter in-laws. Her only knife she had used for several years was misplaced when she moved to her new residence but the grandson told me that they threw it away when they found it. She blames the newcomer health providers who she says torture the girls by circumcising them in the evening under the light of a torch. She acknowledges that there were several cases of over bleeding but blamed it on mothers who were not faithful to their husbands as being the cause for bleeding. Girls who bled were given hard crumbs, *amagoko*, to eat. For severe bleeding, the girl was given her mother's waist beads (love beads) to wear or had the thighs tied with dry banana fibres and or the victim was made to lie with head facing down hill. She also said that despite of frequent bleeding, not many deaths were reported. Despite the side effects, she pitied uncircumcised women by saying *'Ninki mogochandera abana iga?'*: Why do you subject girls to this indecent style of not circumcising them?

Clare Omanga is wife to a renowned politician and former cabinet minister Honourable Andrew Omanga (deceased) of Borabu Division Nyamira district. She was the first Gusii girl to be admitted to Loreto High school in Limuru in 1955, a prestigious national school in Kenya. She has worked as a secretary and in air line services before she joined politics becoming the first lady mayor to Kisii town. She is a chair lady to a woman grass root Women organisation, Maendeleo Ya Wanawake. She has also written storybooks for primary schools.

When I interviewed her on 21st January 2001 at her home, she was totally against female circumcision and even her face showed it. At her school, Loreto, she was the only one in the whole school that was circumcised as she hailed from Gusii where the practice is and has been rampant. During circumcision, she was a victim of over bleeding. She lost a lot of blood and almost lost her life. She was embarrassed all her days at school for being circumcised for her teachers and students saw circumcision as torture and a barbaric act of female circumcision. Soon after her school she swore not to circumcise her daughters who she proudly says never underwent female circumcision. She was blessed with three daughters, who are holding senior positions, a banker, architecture and an interior designer. She advocates for total elimination of the female circumcision practice. She has and will be campaigning against the practice. She has had an opportunity to attend international conferences and has been able to air her views against female circumcision in Gusii.

She has been campaigning against female circumcision at local and international forums where she has presented the Gusii female circumcision practice and why the practice should be eliminated. She has attended among others conferences at Addis Ababa in Ethiopia, Beijing China, Harare, Zimbabwe and United Nations Conference on status on women. She said that the practice of female circumcision undermines the dignity of women apart from being harmful and outdated.

Alexander Onchera Nyoriro is a retired teacher and administrator from Omwari Sub location, Riana Location, Bonchari Suneka Division Central Kisii District

Mr. Alexander Onchera is in his early 70s and a retired teacher and administrator. He is proud to be identified as Omogusii, one who hails from Gusii. He feels that female circumcision should continue so as to maintain Gusii culture and identity. There are four main stages in Gusii culture, birth, circumcision, marriage and death. In the four stages there are also different rites of passages. He believes that female circumcision reduces libido in girls and hence become 'manageable' (not enjoying sex freely even with a spouse). He also feels that female circumcision is mandatory in Gusii. He recalls that any uncircumcised woman married to Gusii was to be 'cut' during birth or if she died before being cut, a cow was given to someone to cut the corpse.

The dead body of uncircumcised female would not be buried before being circumcised. *Egesagane*, the name for an uncircumcised woman, is a derogatory title and provoking to Gusii women. As long as the attitude on *Egesagane* is not changed female circumcision will continue.

Female circumcision was carried out using one knife, blade or a sharp instrument for all clients. When I asked Onchera what he would say about the HIV/AIDS scourge. He did not take serious consideration of side effects during and after circumcision nor clients contracting HIV/AIDS but said the disease does not discriminate. He admits that traditional circumcisers in Bonchari are extinct and there are no girls knowledgeable in rituals, *chinyangi*, that would be trainers of the newly circumcised girls. He also admitted that to some extent in Bonchari some of the circumcision ritual as *esuguta*, keeping a ritual fire and *esubo*, are unheard of. The age of circumcision is lowered to six and after circumcision the candidates may not necessarily become women or adults he admitted.

Hon Catherine Nyamato — former Member of Parliament

Mrs. Catherine Nyamato is married to a prominent Senior Civil Servant and lives at Nyansiongo Settlement Scheme. She is a successful business lady and commands respect from the community as was revealed during the last Parliamentary campaigns.

It is documented that during an anti-female circumcision motion in parliament, she did not support it but in her contribution to the motion, she was in favour of circumcising females. Soon after she lost her seat in parliament she has since changed her mind and is against female circumcision. Mrs. Nyamato who hails from Gusii had strong feelings for circumcising girls as a Gusii woman.

She has lately solicited funds and conducted several seminars against female circumcision in Nyamira district. She is a chairperson to the Federation of Nyamira Women Groups which are campaigning for the elimination of female circumcision among other projects. In her opening remarks during the opening of one of the seminars she said that "the initiates do not have a clear knowledge on what happens during circumcision and she laments on the continuity of the harmful and outdated practice." Uncircumcised girls can grow up and hold or perform prestigious duties, she said, as female circumcision is man made that undermines women's dignity.

Wilkista K. Onsando — former Chairperson, Maendeleo Ya Wanawake Organisation

Wilkista K. Onsando was born and grew up in Gusii under a strong SDA Christian background. She is married to Mr. Mamboleo Onsando, a renowned politician and now lives at Mekenene, Borabu division in Nyamira District. She was trained as a teacher and taught in several schools before she joined Maendeleo Ya Wanawake, a national Women's development organisation where she was an Executive Officer for six years and Chairperson for ten years. She is against female circumcision and has been fighting to eradicate the practice that she says is, 'Outdated, harmful and that does not serve any useful purpose for women in the ever changing world.' She is blessed with three daughters who she did not offer for circumcision.

The husband's side opposed her idea of not circumcising her daughters but with the support of her loving husband and her parents, she succeeded in not circumcising them, an act she is very proud of to date. Her three daughters hold responsible positions, a Finance Executive, Tours and Hotel manager the last one is a successful lawyer.

During her tenure of office with Maendeleo Ya Wanawake, she diplomatically fought against female circumcision, solicited funds to carry research on female circumcision, locally and internationally. She attended anti-female circumcision seminars and also facilitated similar seminars advocating for total elimination of female circumcision. She also made aware the international community the Gusii version of female circumcision and why it should be stopped. The conferences she attended among others include Conference on Population and Development - Dakar Senegal, UN Conference on Population and Development, Cairo Egypt, Ottawa in Canada, Britain and Beijing China.

She also initiated a research on female circumcision in four districts: Kisii, Narok, Meru and Samburu. From the research useful literature, pamphlets and documentation were produced and the said communities gave a clear picture on what female circumcision is in their environment and its implications.

She observes that apart from common side effects of female circumcision, circumcised women in their married life retire from active marital sex early even before menopause.

She said that some Gusii men claim that they get sexual satisfaction from uncircumcised women preferably Luo and Luhyia but only goes to their spouses in making babies. Parents do not have any right to decide on their daughter's sex life, how to have it or how much of it they should have. Gusii women were being circumcised to tame women sexually and also reduce their libido. She appeals for education and intensive community awareness on side effects of female circumcision. Mothers in-law should not to interfere with young couples who decide not to circumcise their daughters. All unmarried men should be encouraged to marry 'whole women' really women, uncircumcised women. For girls she says do not undergo circumcision, say NO to female circumcision.

Pacifica Kemunto Mochoge — female circumciser from Bosamaro Chache, Tinga Market, is a third wife of a former military officer in the 1st World War, Mr. Machogu Matanga of Bosamaro Chache Location, Nyamira District. She claims to hail from a lineage of female circumcisers, grandmother and cousin on the mother's side were among the famous circumcisers. She remembers how the ancestral spirits called her to be a circumciser. One time in life, she fell sick, very sick vomiting with poor health. Whenever she was taken to hospital, no cause of sickness was detected. A disease requires many herbs, she said, *"nchogu neya 'mete 'menge"*. She finally turned to a fortune teller to find out what exactly was happening to her health. The fortune teller predicted that the cause of her sickness was a requirement to become a community female circumciser. She was asked to fulfill an ancestral requirement of sacrificing goats. After slaughtering the ninth one, a blacksmith was asked to make a sacred knife for the purpose of circumcision in 1954, the only knife she has ever used since then and in her custody as I write. After slaughtering a tenth goat, jingles (*chindege*) were made by a blacksmith. On receipt of the sacred items, she was ready to circumcise. The first client was her own daughter and then followed by other girls from the community.

When I interviewed her, she admitted that after circumcision, most girls over bled to an extent that the women became

Notable female circumciser Pacifica Kemunto Mochoge
of Ting'a, Nyamira County

helpless. She provided a kind of medicine, *rirongo*, which could not be helpful in stopping bleeding at times. She claims that many women who are health providers have joined the business for monetary gains against the wishes of ancestors. She claims that levy charged for circumcision was only used in buying food and if possible build a living house after many years of saving. She further says that the newcomers (female circumcisers) have no ancestral calling. They circumcise girls in the evenings using floodlights or torches and want to increase their financial income. She is not in favour of stopping female circumcision practice for it is the ancestral forces which require circumcision to be done and therefore should be obeyed.

Hochi Oenga Biari— traditional male circumcisor
Hochi Oenga hails from Bogichora and is in the line of male circumcisers after his father Paul Biari. Addressing an anti-female circumcision seminar at Kebabe in December 1998, he condemned female circumcision and said that his younger daughters are whole without the 'cut' but encourages male circumcision under good and hygienic environment.

Charles Mochibi Sindani — Famous traditional male circumciser
He is the latest male circumciser who hails from Bonyamatuta sub location, Gucha Location Nyamira District. His father, Rabachi was a famous male circumciser that was nick named Sindani (needle) because he circumcised many boys and many people teased him of making many needles. Charles who attained primary education condemns female circumcision but recommends boys' circumcision under hygienic conditions and not using one knife as he and his late father did.

Mr. Nelson Manduku Mokong'u— retired Chief and teacher of East Kitutu location
Mr. Nelson Manduku Mokong'u, Retired Chief and teacher of East Kitutu location is also in favour of awareness seminars on side effects of female circumcision. He acknowledges that until he attended an anti-female circumcision seminar he was green and never knew what happened exactly during the circumcision and its immediate and long-term negative implications. He said in Kiswahili that *"Kutia wasichana chandoni ni mila na desturi ambayo imepitwa na wakati"* (female circumcision is outdated).

Demba Diawara — an Imam from Senegal

The same sentiments of attending awareness seminars has been sounded by Demba Diawara an Imam from Senegal who said "Men need to learn about the danger this practice presents to the health of women, and about human rights to be more open minded. They have to understand that stopping this practice (FGM) will improve the health of their women and children, and is important to their survival." (Man Power, Volume 3, issue 3 September 1999, as indicated in Awaken magazine distributed by EQUALITY NOW)

Chapter Eight
Efforts Towards Eradication of Female Circumcision

World Health Organisation (WHO)

The World Health Organisation (WHO) has 47 member countries in Africa where Kenya is one of them. Relevant resolutions of the WHO Regional Committee for Africa and the World Health Assembly have been reached as referred in the Resolution paper- AFR/RC39/R9 concerning traditional Practices affecting women and children.

Considering the adverse effects on maternal and child health in certain traditional practices such as female circumcision, early marriage, nutritional taboos and such practices,

Considering the high priority given by WHO and member states to maternal and Child health,

Convinced that WHO has an important role to play in control of traditional practices affecting maternal and child health,

1. Recommends that the member states concerned:

i) Adopt appropriate policies and strategies to eliminate female circumcision

ii) Organize educational and informational activities bearing in mind local cultural contexts, in order to create awareness among women and men of the dangers of female circumcision.... Inform general public of the possible relationship between the propagation of infectious diseases including AIDS and female circumcision

iii) Prohibit the medicalization of female circumcision and discourage health personnel from performing this operation

iv) Include in training programme for health personnel and traditional Birth Attendants relevant information to dangers of female circumcision

v) Encourage research projects to identify the most effective means of controlling these practices.

vi) Take the steps necessary to put into practice the various recommendations made at the national level and international levels in this area.

Any work that has been done in Kenya to eliminate female circumcision by SDA Rural Health services, PATH Kenya, *Maendeleo Ya Wanawake Organisation* and other non-governmental organizations has been on voluntary basis without a national policy on female circumcision. (National plan of Action for elimination of Female circumcision in Kenya 1999-2019) document of June 1999.

It is surprising to learn that Kenya lacks government policy or legislation on female circumcision though it is a member of WHO which is against Female Genital Mutilation in the African region. This has constrained female circumcision elimination efforts. The government of Kenya however is a signatory to the international convention that addresses Female circumcision. The issue of Female Circumcision needs to be addressed in relevant government sectoral policies and legislation that support female circumcision eradication.

The process of such addresses has begun and will be greatly enhanced by Regional plan of action.

Ministry of Health & Plan of action against Female Circumcision

The the Minister for Public Health[1] in the Republic of Kenya Hon. Sam Ongeri said that diplomacy approach will be applied in the efforts of eliminating female genital mutilation practice as opposed to prosecution against those who practice and impose female circumcision. ('Daily Nation', Thursday, November 18, 1999). He is in view that if the government and its machinery prosecute offenders, it will cause the painful practice to go "underground". The government has launched a twenty year (-1999 - 2019) national plan of action aimed at accelerating the elimination of female circumcision. All those who will be

---

1 As of going to press Sam Ongeri was Minister for Foreign Affairs

implementing activities geared towards the elimination of the practice will use a plan of action document as a guiding tool. The Kenya Demographic Health Survey (1998) Prof. Ongeri observed that women from the tribes of Luo and Abaluhyia female circumcision is rare. However FGM among Abagusii women aged 15 - 19 is nearly universal of 97% and lowest among the Miji Kenda/ Swahili tribes 12%.

He said that the objectives of the national plan of action include:

- To reduce the number of girls and women who undergo any type of FGM
- To increase the proportion of communities supporting the elimination of FGM through positive changes in attitudes, beliefs, behaviour and practices
- To increase the proportion of primary, secondary and tertiary health care facilities that provide care, counselling and support to girls and women possessing physical and psychological problems associated with FGM and
- To increase the technical and advocacy capacity of institutions, agencies and communities in development, implementation and management of FGM and elimination programmes.

It is worth to note that Professor Sam Ongeri hails from Gusii where female circumcision is rampant and resistant to change. He also knows how deeply the practice is rooted and the implication of the uncircumcised girls or women.

The Seventh Day Adventist church stand on FGM

The Seventh Day Adventist Church is on the forefront to see that the Female circumcision is eradicated. The message to its followers and people of good will the SDA Church has this to say: "Because female genital mutilation threatens physical, emotional, and relational health, Seventh Day Adventists are opposed to this practice. The church calls on its health care professionals, educational and medical institutions, and all members along with people of good will to cooperate in efforts to eliminate the practice of female genital mutilation. Through education and loving presentation of the gospel, it is our hope and our intention that those threatened by the practice will find protection and wholeness and that those who have been subjected to this practice will find solace and compassionate care" (page 137 - Statements, Guidelines and other documents of SDA Church General Conference- June 2000)

The Adventist Church's opposition to female genital mutilation is based on the f Biblical principles of preservation of life and health, blessing of marital intimacy, healthful procreation, protection of vulnerable persons (under age, young girl), compassionate care, sharing truth and respect of cultures.

In Gusii where the female circumcision is rampant and has resisted change, the SDA Church took a firm stand against the practice. A committee chaired by Nathan O. Ogeto was held on 29/10/1986 at Nyanchwa whereby they prayed and buried female circumcision in Gusii and Narok. The committee later involved church leaders, (Dorcas), SDA Church women, church workers, medical practitioners, civil servants and the abagusii community to join hands to eradicate the harmful practice. Also attending the meeting included W. Matoya, J. Manani, S. Nyachieo, W. Mochama, E. Mayieng'a, J. Messophirr, S. Nyachieng'a, D. Sinkira, J. Mokaya, C.Nyantika and A. Ateka.

Further to these efforts for a good cause, the SDA church obtained a Circular letter Ref. MED/10/11/4 dated 13th November 1990 from the Acting Kisii District Commissioner, Mr. L. S. Ngaluma. The circular, with enough copies to District Officers, chiefs and Assistant chiefs had a message to support the SDA church in disseminating information on the side effects of female circumcision practice.

The president His Excellency Daniel Arap Moi and Grace Ogot an Assistant Minister of Social services had given strong statements appearing in the Kenya Times December, 30th 1989 and an article of 6.6 1990 against female circumcision.

Catholic Church Stand on Female Circumcision

As a result of AIDS epidemics, the Catholic Church is making an effort to enlighten everyone to live AIDS free life. The church is advising youth to be at the helm to lead us all away from certain traditions which have long ceased to be useful and which are in fact down right dangerous - including female circumcision (clitoridectomy and infibulation) as indicated in the Pastoral letter of the Catholic Bishops in Kenya, page 7, of December 1999.

In the hierarchy of the Catholic Church Bishops and those who are above this level have authority to speak for the Catholic Church. When I spoke to a Priest in charge of a local parish who declined to be quoted, but gave me his own personal view on what he thought about female circumcision in Gusii where he happens to come from. As he was growing up and living with his family, he did not know the side effects of female circumcision until he attended anti-female circumcision seminars some organized by the Seventh Day Adventist Church as an observer. He feels that to eradicate the deeply rooted culture and practice of female circumcision in Gusii is not easy but will be gradual. It is a joint venture where everyone should be involved. He also advocates for several anti female circumcision seminars to all persons from all walks of life in Gusii. He appeals for an acceptable Alternative Rite of Passage whereby actual circumcision will be avoided.

He cited examples where female circumcision is done secretly which will make the practice live longer than anticipated. He shares with his Parish believers the side effects of female circumcision in his personal capacity since his seniors will only deliver the statement concerning the same.

Efforts to Eliminate Female Circumcision in Nyamira District

I returned from Mogadishu, Somalia after working for three years as a Global Missionary for the Seventh Day Adventist Church. When I was away in Mogadishu, I became inspired and swore to do everything humanly possible to eradicate female circumcision. I had an opportunity of reading about side effects of the female circumcision practice in Senegal, Somalia, Ethiopia, Sierra Leone and other developed countries with large numbers of immigrants. The more I read about FGM, the more I hated the practice.

On arrival in Nyamira, my home district, I joined Mr. Johnson Masimba, Mrs. Pauline Mogeni and Mr. David Omare from Nyamira Adventist Medical Centre as a volunteer Project Coordinator a volunteer. This was a team of four dedicated persons from Nyamira Adventist Medical Centre that was campaigning against female circumcision which is rampant and resistant to change in the district. The team mobilized and sensitized Abagusii community in Nyamira district against female circumcision.

They were out to eradicate the female circumcision in the district. Mr. Johnson Masimba and Mr. David Omare started from their families by not circumcising their daughters and declaring it in public, but opted to send them to a seminar on Alternative Rite of Passage which was planned in December 1998 at Kebabe in Nyamira district. Alternative rite of passage which is a process of preparing girls into womanhood without actual "the cut" was encouraged as opposed to obware. A similar Alternative Rite of Passage has been carried out in Meru with success but not relevant to the Gusii culture.

This campaign against female circumcision was done on a voluntary basis by the said four members and on part-time basis during weekends and free time. Thanks to Mr. Josephat Nyagero of African Medical Research Foundation (AMREF), Nyamira branch, who provided a generator, a television and video cassette recorder to be used during the campaign. The members of Seventh Day Adventist Church provided transport, meals and accommodation for the facilitators. The campaigns were very successful and well attended. I am also grateful to Station Pastors, Chiefs and Assistant Chiefs who invited the people to attend the campaigns where the facilitators had a forum to address the issue of Anti-Female Circumcision but encouraged the Alternative Rite of Passage.

During the Anti-Female Circumcision campaigns the facilitators visited the following places in Nyamira District which were well attended: Riakworo, Nyakongo, Mong'oni, Nyambaria, Tinderet, Sironga, Kebabe, Gesiaga, Kenyambi, Kebirigo, Nyamusi, Nyamira Technical Secondary School, Gekano High School, Kiabonyoru, Kenyenya, Bonyunyu, Ekerenyo, Menyenya. The Anti-Female Circumcision campaign was well supported by the church workers especially Pastor Stanely Nyachieng'a Barini who was very instrumental and a member of the first committee in the SDA church that vowed to eradicate the female circumcision practice. The response to avoiding actual 'cutting' was positive, successful and applauded by parents and the initiates. As a result of the campaign, 441 girls were later sent to Kebabe Girls' High School to attend a two weeks seclusion seminar on *Alternative Rite of Passage*. The 441 girls had been prepared to undergo female circumcision during the December holiday of 1998 but opted for NO CUT but attend *Alternative Rite of Passage* seminar.

After I realized this response I knew that ahead of me were many girls were set to come to attend this pioneer seminar. The volunteer team had no funds to conduct the seminar. I wrote a proposal and approached Maendeleo Ya Wanawake, Ford Foundation. PATH Kenya, Japanese Embassy, SDA Church and Rainbo of New York soliciting for funds. As time of circumcision was running out the volunteer team was promised funding from Rainbo New York through Ford Foundation, PATH Kenya and the SDA church. Funds were required to cater for transport and per diem of facilitators, accommodation, stationery, certificates and gifts for the initiates which is an integral part in female circumcision for Abagusii, *obware.*

Chapter Nine
Alternative Rite of Passage

In the previous chapters I have shown how Gusii female circumcision was done and how complicated it is with many detailed activities, rites and rituals. The practice is deeply rooted such that any effort made to change or eradicate it, is immediately met with opposition from Gusii community. Changing or eliminating the female circumcision practice is likened to dealing with an addicted smoker to stop smoking, an alcoholic person to stop drinking or weaning a baby and introducing him/her to more solid foods. For an alcoholic to stop drinking an addicted smoker to stop smoking and a baby to stop the mother's milk the process is gradual and a lot of patience is required. To realize success to stop a deeply rooted practice, alternatives should be provided. For a smoker something to engage the mouth as a sweet is suggested. For a baby mashed potatoes and porridge will do, and for an alcoholic avoiding former beer places and friends are possible alternatives.

After seeing the significance of female circumcision practice in Gusii, it will not be eliminated or changed as when a driver applies emergency brakes and the vehicle complies and stops. A relevant and acceptable alternative should be suggested or provided. The following is the nature of Abagusii people as rightly mentioned by Nehemiah Nyaundi in his book *Seventh Day Adventism in Gusii, Kenya* (page 42):

"Culturally, the Abagusii are not a type that ventures into the unknown. They like to take their time. And of course their concept of time is the generous one; such as what can be done tomorrow can wait."

I would like to suggest alternatives of the whole process of female circumcision that has four main parts Preparation, Actual Circumcision, Seclusion, Graduation and Final Handing over of the initiates to the community. Since Abagusii agree that culture is not static, *makoro magoti nande achicha*, it is my hope that the Alternative Rite of Passage will be acceptable.

Preparation

Preparation of initiates took several months before actual circumcision. During the preparation period, the initiate was being prepared psychologically and physically. Enough firewood to keep the ritual fire was collected and enough food, beer was arranged for.

Suggested Alternative

Seminars for both parents and initiates are encouraged. The topics will include side effects of female circumcision and get prepared to attend a residential seminar to elaborate on what obware entails.

Actual circumcision

During the period of actual circumcision, women were invited to take the initiate the circumcisor for actual circumcision. Teacher and trainer, *omosegi*, was identified by the parents before circumcision. The parents to feed the participants and the invited guests provided a lot of food, locally brewed beer and meat. The proverb, *ekiomogoko nomwana ogetoire*, suggests that because of the initiate, even the mean family will provide food to the participants and the community. The father of the initiate and his friends witnessed the daughter enter the main house for training and learning. Friends and relatives gave additional food stuffs, egetoro.

Suggested alternative

In the Alternative Rite of Passage, actual circumcision should be stopped since we have learnt that it is not necessary to make a woman an adult or mature. The side effects of female circumcision both immediate and long term are to be avoided if actual circumcision is not performed. Parents can select a teacher and trainer, *omosegi* for their daughter who will accompany her to the residential centre for an Alternative Rite of Passage seminar. Donations of additional food stuffs from friends and relatives, *egetoro,* will be encouraged and providing food to participants and invited guests is welcome, *echae ya morero.* The father and his friends will witness his daughter being escorted to the residential centre for Alternative Rite of Passage.

Seclusion

Seclusion period during the actual Gusii female circumcision, obware took from five to ten weeks. Seclusion period was the time of Education, learning and training. Teacher and trainer, omosegi, women and girls did all the training and teaching of the newly circumcised girl. Topics for training included laundry, simple botany, cookery, reproduction, procreation, sex, being responsible, taking care of items, on becoming a woman and being industrious tough and brave. Seclusion period was also for healing and hiding from the community.

Suggested Alternative

For seclusion, the girls will attend a residential seminar for one week away from home. The initiates will be accompanied with their teacher and trainer. Women both circumcised and uncircumcised from Gusii will facilitate during the seminar. Additional topics will be HIV/AIDS, sexually transmitted diseases, simple hygiene, and great women in the Bible, Gusii and Kenya. Rites and rituals, *chinyangi* will be optional. Girls of circumcision age are between 6 and 12 years old. For the purpose of effective learning, the girls will be divided into two groups, girls aged between 6 and 9 and the other group girls aged between 10 and 12.

Graduation

Graduation period in the actual rite of passage is short and few activities are carried out involving few members of the family. Parents blesses the newly graduated candidate, grandmother burns plants used as a bed, *amabuko* and the girls witness the washing of the newly graduated candidate and finally handed over to the community for additional responsibilities, duties and roles. New clothes and exchange of gifts becomes the integral part of graduation.

Suggested Alternative:

Graduation at the Alternative Rite of Passage ceremony is expected to be brief and colourful. Songs, drama, plays and poems will be encouraged. Parents, community leaders, politicians and government officials will be invited to attend to witness the graduation of 'whole' girls. Certificates of graduation will be awarded and prayers and blessings will be conducted. Exchange of gifts and new dresses for the newly graduated girls will be carried out and finally the graduates will be handed over to the community, chiefs, church elders and clan elders.

Since the Alternative rite of passage will be an annual event, committees are to be established to plan for the following year.

Awareness female circumcision campaigns

Since Abagusii are not a type that ventures into the unknown, awareness campaigns and seminars are required to prepare them to venture into Alternative Rite of Passage from childhood into womanhood. In Abagusii proverb, *makoro magoti nande achicha*, they accept that culture is not static but changes with time. The changes and positive results are likely to have a greater impact if conducted and facilitated by Abagusii for Abagusii themselves.

Whenever anti-female circumcision seminars have been conducted by persons from outside Gusiiland, Abagusii community feels that a foreign tradition and culture is being introduced and imposed on them. Gusii men do not know in details.

Most men from Gusii do not know exactly what happens during female circumcision, the negative and harmful effects the innocent girl of a tender age undergoes. Enlightening seminars and campaigns on side effects of female circumcision should be encouraged for men, women, youths and the girls under 12 years who are prepared for the "cruel knife" of the circumcisor. My late father Mzee Mokaya Ong'ayo of Bonyaikoma East Kitutu location who died at the age of over 90 years had his twelve daughters circumcised; seven of my own mother and five stepsisters. I observed him keenly each year whenever my sisters underwent circumcision. He was not worried of the side effects of the practice but implemented what was required of him as a father of the circumcised girls. May be he did know of any immediate and long term side effects or he did not want to think about them since his own sisters and mother had undergone the circumcision. Instead he provided enough food to participants, locally brewed beer, *amarwa*, to old men, witnessed the daughters enter the main house for teaching and training during the seclusion period and blessed them during graduation. Without enlightenment from Raha and Khadija on side effects of female circumcision while I was working in Mogadishu as a global missionary, I would have not been even better than my late loving father nor would I be thinking differently on female circumcision and writing this book for the eradication of female circumcision practice.

Women are actively and directly involved during the Gusii female circumcision session. Actual circumcision for girls is not done by men but by women only. Women also do teaching and training of initiates. In the *Alternative Rite of Passage into Womanhood*, Abagusii women should be trained as Trainers Of Trainees on the alternative practice and thereafter facilitate in seminars aimed at eradicating female circumcision practice. Along with circumcised, uncircumcised women (who will be models to be emulated), health providers that have recently started to circumcise girls should be invited to attend such seminars. Traditional birth attendants, female circumcisors, women leaders and women pastors should also attend in order to have great impact and success.

Rights of the Girl Child

Youth in and out of school should also be made aware of the Rights of the child, adopted by the General Assembly of the United Nations on 20 November 1989, child abuse, legislation on children in Kenya and the side effects of female circumcision. For this matter, boys should be prepared to marry 'whole' girls in future as opposed to circumcised ones.

Girls aged between six and twelve are vulnerable in the female circumcision practice. They should be aware of what is entailed in female circumcision, immediate and long-term side effects of the practice. After being enlightened, they should learn to say "NO CUT" for the sake of their health and their decision should be respected. See article 12 of convention on the rights of the child:

1. States parties shall assure to the child who is capable of forming his or her own views the right to express those views freely in all matters affecting the child, the views of the child being given due weight in accordance with the age and maturity of the child.

2. For this purpose, the child shall in particular be provided an opportunity to be heard in any judicial and administrative proceedings affecting the child, either directly, or through a representative or an appropriate body, in a manner consistent with the procedural rules of a national Law.

Heads of learning institutions are encouraged to take an initiative to protect girls from being circumcised, harassed, embarrassed or humiliated because of their decision or state of not being circumcised.

The female circumcision, *obware,* amongst Abagusii peoples in Kenya is deeply rooted and has resisted change leave alone eradication of the practice. The Kenya Demographic Health Survey (1998) showed that 38% of Kenyan women had undergone the female circumcision practice that involves the cutting of the female genitalia. The survey further shows that among Abagusii women aged 15-19 is nearly universal (97%)

and other Kenyan tribes is lower and others like Abaluyia and Luo Female Circumcision is rare.

Other tribes the survey showed that: female circumcision is very common among the Maasai (89%), Kalenjin (62%), Taita/ Taveta (59%), Meru and Embu groups (54%), lower percentages of Kikuyu (43%), Kamba (33%) and Miji Kenda/ Swahili (12%).

Looking at the above statistics, it reflects that Abagusii have the highest percentage of circumcised women in Kenya. In the early sixties the rate was high amongst the Kikuyu as Ngugi Wa Thiong'o seems to suggest in his book, The River Between. It was the time when women wanted to be women, circumcised women. It was a time when the society was torn apart between culture and the coming of Christianity; the time of fighting harmful culture while embracing development and useful foreign ideas. In 1998 the rate of circumcised Kikuyu women fell lower than that of the Maasai, Kalenjin and Abagusii. Some of the reasons of low rate include enlightenment of female circumcision side effects, positive change of attitudes, beliefs and life style.

Though slow and gradual, the attitude of Abagusii towards *egesagane*, uncircumcised girl or woman should be changed positively. Luhyia and Luo women for example are not circumcised but they are not viewed the same way as uncircumcised girl or woman from Gusii. There is an inner feeling within Abagusii men to accept uncircumcised from elsewhere than from Gusii itself.

The word *egesagane* is derogatory, abusive and provoking once used on a circumcised woman from Gusii. It is common to see a woman from Gusii ready to fight to defend her title of circumcision if provoked by uncircumcised woman. So the word *egesagane* should not be used or limit its use.

Rites and rituals associated with rite of passage, including circumcision, *chinyangi*, are held to be sacred by Abagusii people. They are not to be revealed to anyone who has not undergone circumcision and its rituals. Even some Christians, church Pastors included, will not be comfortable to narrate to a foreigner what rites and rituals they underwent during *obware*. For this reason, I have taken the opportunity to write what happened during *obware* so that the circumcised and the uncircumcised alike will read the facts and see for themselves what happened.

When the facts, procedure and significance of female circumcision are documented, there will be no secret and any illusions on the rites and rituals, *chinyangi*.

Chapter Ten
Social and Cultural Woes of Female Circumcision

Culture is not static as the case always is. Among the Abagusii there have been painfully slow changes in OBWARE for girls - [Rite of passage from childhood into adulthood] the following have contributed to these changes:

Mixed marriages- Abagusii men have married from people who do not circumcise girls or circumcise boys under different customs, beliefs tradition and culture. When the couple of this type bears children they have different opinions on under what tradition and how to circumcise they own children or to circumcise or not circumcise females. This applies to Abagusii women are or married outside the Abagusii community.

Education, Christianity and awareness- both men and woman from Gusii who have had high Education and attended seminars and workshop or have been converted Christians change their attitudes, behaviour in cultures and traditions that are harmful especially female circumcision. They do not feel bound and committed to such harmful cultures and traditions. Elite and converted Christians people circumcised their male children in hospitals avoiding many rituals as demanded by Abagusii culture and avoid circumcising girls. Culturally it is very challenging for pioneers who declare and avoid female circumcision. The first ritual omitted or excluded from *obware* was keeping the ritual fire alive during circumcision period of seclusion.

Migration— some Abagusii people have migrated from the rural Gusii land to urban centres and foreign countries in search of jobs, business, and higher education. Others have settled in other areas in Kenya away from Gusii land. As they live outside the Gusii environment they adapt urban living styles and hence loss Abagusii identity, its traditions and culture and customs including Obware for girls with its rites and rituals.

Preparation for circumcision is very involving and much money is used during the month of December. Many relatives and friends are invited for feasting, merry making in the homes where circumcision is expected to be carried out. There is a lot of food, beer and gifts are purchased and at times people take loans to fulfil their dream of feeding the multitude. Even the poorest people and the mean are expected to provide food to the community during circumcision period.

In December each year which is a Circumcision period many women including traditional birth attendants, women hospital support staff, nurses (generally but wrongly referred to as Sister - 'trained nurses') pose as circumcisors and make arrangements with rural communities with middlemen and travel to rural areas to perform the outdated female circumcision in places with little hygiene. A traditional circumcisor who I spoke to said that she has lost her circumcision work to women who are known to be working in hospitals or private clinics. Some parents belief that these women know what should be done as they work in medical or clinical places. In contrary it should be clear that in the Nursing Training syllabus, the subject of female circumcision is NOT included which means that any nurse performing female circumcision is doing it at her own risk and against medical ethics. A fee ranging from Ksh. 200-500 ($ 3-6) is chargeable to each girl undergoing circumcision.

There have been cases of embarrassment to circumcised women from Gusii. When they are asked to confirm that they are circumcised, they often deny avoiding being embarrassed. I would therefore suggest that total eradication of female circumcision in Gusiiland is due to keep up well with the fast changing world. It should also be understood that there are several Gusii women who are not circumcised but fulfill all requirements as elite women and real women who lack nothing as women. They hold responsible positions in private offices, civil service, parastatals and even non governmental organisations. They get married, give birth to children, and manage their families well contrary to the Abagusii beliefs.

Obware - (Female circumcision, rites and rituals) in itself will not make a 6 year old a woman. Obware is meant to be a rite of passage from childhood to womanhood. Girls in Gusii should learn to have self-confidence and know that their parents and the community will love them even in the way they are and not necessarily through circumcision.

It is my hope that the bill presented in parliament will become a law and as such female circumcision will be outlawed in the Republic of Kenya. This will give Gusii men who refuse to marry from Gusii a chance to marry Abagusii women along with others of their choice. Hopefully the system of secretly circumcising girls is likely to stop and hence celebrate the eradication of Female circumcision. Meanwhile I encourage all persons to get involved in eradicating the outdated and inhuman practice.

In October 1994, as a response to the call to Global Action, UNICEF issued an executive directive declaring that female circumcision is a health hazard to children and violation of their human rights. In 1979 at the World Health Organization's seminar on Traditional Practices affecting the health of women and children, Dr. A.H. Taba, former Regional Director of the WHO Eastern Mediterranean Region, made the following statement concerning the health risks of female circumcision FGM:

"it is self-evident that any form of surgical interference in the highly sensitive genital organs constitutes a serious threat to the child, and that the painful operation is a source of major physical as well as psychological trauma. The extent and nature of the immediate and long- term mental disturbances will depend on the child's inner defences, the prevailing psychological environment, and a host of other factors. The family no doubt does its best to mitigate the painful effects of the operation; nonetheless, the child necessarily undergoes an overwhelming experience.

Even before the operation, the threat of 'cutting' and [the] fear - provoking situation may disturb the mental state of the child to the degree [that] it causes worry, anxiety, sleeplessness, nightmares or panic. As anticipatory precautions against these anxieties, the family commonly uses various forms of traditional magico-religious practice such as fumigation, or the wearing of amulets."

Culture is not static but keeps on changing with time, environment and scientific finding. In a Gusii proverb *makoro magoti nande achicha*. Soon after Christianity was introduced in Gusiiland, there have been some changes in custom, taboo, tradition and culture. Harmful practices have been dropped altogether but eradicating the practice of female circumcision has been painfully slow and is resistant in Gusiiland.

The eating of blood, wearing animal skins, hunting wild animals for food and making a living, women not eating chicken are some of the taboos and customs that have been abandoned. As far as actual physical female circumcision is concerned, many parents circumcise their daughters but leave out some rites and rituals as: keeping the ritual fire alive, *esuguta* and *chinyangi*. I am appealing for Alternative Rite of Passage whereby there is no actual circumcision rites and rituals can be kept if need be.

At some point in the circumcision song encourages sexual intercourse to the circumcised so long as it is done by circumcised men. (*orenge mokabaisia obeire mokabamura*) This is dangerous to the young girls for they feel that they are at the top of the world and can make love as they wish. Unwanted pregnancies, HIV/AIDS will result to those endangered people.

Female Circumcision — in the Koran and Bible

By all means female circumcision has no backing in the Bible nor in the Koran teachings and hence Christians and Moslems alike should not circumcise their daughters. There is no major Islamic citation that makes female circumcision a religious requirement. Neither the Koran nor the "Hadith" which are collections of the sayings of the prophet Mohamed recorded from oral histories after his death, include a direct call for female circumcision. Not only there is no specific call for female circumcision in the Quran, but the procedure is not practiced in predominantly Islamic countries such as Saudi Arabia, Iraq, the Gulf States, Kuwait, Algeria and Pakistan.

In fact, people from Muslim countries that do not practice female circumcision react with surprise when they hear about it and find it difficult to believe that female circumcision is linked to Islam as they know it. (Page 31, 32 FGM a call for global action by Nahid Toubia).

Bible

•Genesis 17: 10 this is my convent, which ye shall keep, between me and you and thy seed after thee; Every man child among you shall be circumcised (KJV). God further gave instruction how circumcision was to be physically done to only men.

•Genesis 17: 15 And God said unto Abraham, as for Sar'rai thy wife, thou shalt not call her name Sa'rai but Sarah shall her name be. Abraham's wife only changed her name and no physical circumcision performed on her. It is also understood that the Prophet Mohammed had four daughters and they did not undergo female circumcision.

Chapter Eleven
Alternative Rite of Passage Seminar

The following is what took place at Kebabe Girls' Secondary school, Alternative Rite of Passage Seminar.

The *Alternative Rite of Passage* is a substitute relevant to - Female Circumcision and its rites and rituals known as *obware.* The simple difference between *obware* and the Alternative rite of passage is that only actual female circumcision is not performed. Other processes of preparation, seclusion and graduation of the girls are carried out in the alternative Rite of Passage with modifications to suit today's environment and standard of living.

The *Alternative Rite of Passage* seminar was scheduled and carried out between 29th November to 13th December 1998 at Kebabe Girls' Secondary School in Nyamira District. It was co-funded by the Seventh Day Adventist Church, Nyamira Conference, Rainbo New York, through Ford Foundation Nairobi and PATH Kenya.

In the first two days the centre received a record of 441 girls who had opted for NO CUT but an *Alternative Rite of Passage* with a motto: *OGOSARWA NOMOYIO YAYA!* (No cut!) with a theme song: — *We are the children of the light,* composed from the book of Ephesians 5:8. The girls, aged from 5 to 14 years, attended the seminar. The residential nurse made a physical check of the girls to ascertain that they all girls attending the seminar had not undergone the female circumcision. I learnt that the mother of the youngest girls ran away with her daughter to the seminar to escape being influenced or forced by the husbands and grand parents to circumcise their daughter. She had clear awareness on negative effects on female circumcision during the anti Female Circumcision campaigns that helped her make a strong decision of not "Cutting" her beloved daughter.

Opening Ceremony

The seminar was privileged and honoured as it was officially opened by Mr. Earnest Munyi the then Nyamira District Commissioner, in attendance of Medical Officer of Health.

Photo by Author: Anti FGM campaigners
at Tindereti in Borabu, Nyamira County

In his opening remarks the District Commissioner said that it is a responsibility of leaders to address female circumcision practice and eliminate it from the community as it was rampant and resistant. Other communities in the country had succeeded in reducing the number of girls being circumcised by involving leaders and the communities involved in female circumcision. He cited health consequences of excessive bleeding, life long psychological trauma and even death of the initiate. He encouraged awareness campaigns so that parents and the community will be able to respect the rights of the child. He totally supported the Alternative rite of passage as it is not harmful to initiates and knowledge gained there is relevant. He felt that *Alternative Rite of Passage* should be made an annual event. All NGOs involved in campaigning against female circumcision should come together and present their programmes to the district development committee so that a universal district programme can be developed to reach more people. He regretted that some health providers have started to have monetary gains from female circumcision making it difficult to eradicate the practice. He further said that it not ethical for health providers to engage in female circumcision. Uncircumcised girls will get suitors and will develop as normal girls as opposed to some distorted traditional beliefs. The fact remains that men prefer to marry uncircumcised girls. He then declared the seminar officially open.

The remarks of the Executive Chairman of the SDA Church Nyamira Conference Pastor Richard Nyakego said that it was time for Abagusii to change and leave harmful culture of female circumcision, which do not have any Biblical backing. The practice though rampant and resistant is outdated and has no place in modern Christian living. The efforts of elimination are a joint effort by all leaders and Christians who form 80% of Abagusii people.

During the opening ceremony the Medical Officer Of Health addressed the participants and gave these remarks. The girls will learn useful information during the two weeks which they will live by in life. He said that health providers that perform female circumcision are money thirsty, have taken advantage of ignorant parents and they are doing female circumcision as individuals and at their own risk. He proposed awareness seminar for them in the future.

He urged seminar coordinator to provide a complete report to his office to help him and his committee to develop a policy and guidelines in the efforts of eliminating the practice.

After the opening ceremony the 441 girls were grouped into age groups for easy training and teaching. The older girls became guides to the young ones with the help of mothers that attended the seminar. Seclusion period was used for training, instruction and guidance. The substituted topics of Obware included: unwanted pregnancies, self esteem, decision making, home economics, women models in the nation and the Bible, simple hygiene, simple Botany, Christian sermons, rites and rituals (Chinyangi), poems, drama, plays and songs. Women taught all these topics. The men who at the centre : Mr. Daniel M. Mokaya coordinated seminar activities, Mr. Johnson Masimba showed films, Mr. David Oyaro kept some accounts and Mr. Lameck Ong'era did video coverage on all activities. The following were seminar facilitators:

1. Pauline Mogeni — centre nurse,
2. Pastor Dorcas Ongaga — residential pastor
3. Fanis Kiage — Home Science secondary school teacher
4. Jeliah Gekara — community and religious advisor
5. Rachel Mogoi — nurse
6. Mary Omare — Community nurse and mother of participant initiate
7. Delilah Mogeni — teacher
8. Rael Bina — mother
9. Ruth Mounde — Deputy Head teacher Kebabe Girls' Secondary school
10. Agnes Apiemi — house wife and rituals (chinyangi) expert
11. Dorcas Obegi — house wife, she was in charge of songs
12. Zephaniah Ongere — Head teacher Kebabe Girls' Secondary school

Other centre facilitators included:

1. Beatrice Siro
2. Josephine Nyanganyi
3. Pricilla Ayuka
4. Rachael Okongo
5. Tabitha Nyanchoka
6. Winfred Momanyi
7. Ruth Kemuma - Typist
8. Wilson Maroko
9. Hezron Okemwa
10. Priscah Akora
11. Esther Kwamboka
12. Yunes Nyarinda
13. Naomi Nyamweya

The following were visiting facilitators from outside Nyamira

Alternative Rite Of Passage coordinator Meru.

2.Inovioleta Mbwari — Peer educator, professional advisory counseling (PAC) Nairobi

3.Sarah Mohamed — Peer Educator Kibera self Help Project Nairobi.

4.Mivajuma Tatu — Peer educator, Slums information and resource centre - Nairobi

5.Mrs. Manyara — South Kenya Conference

During the residential seminar many people who are fighting the total eradication of female circumcision visited the centre. These included Dr. Asha from Washington DC, Dr. Samson Radeny of PATH Kenya Nairobi, several Christian pastors from Gusii, Lucy Mathai consultant sent by Ford Foundation Nairobi, Mrs. Abigael Matini community health provider and aspirant member of Parliament Kitutu East constituency and the area District Officer of Ekerenyo.

On the last day of graduation the girls received new dresses as gifts which is an integral part of Obware. The girls dressed in the their new dresses looked like angels as the marched and sang to the divisional headquarters to be addressed by the District Officer (DO). No one could withstand the powerful voice of a soloist Dorcas Obegi as she led the procession in singing the theme song "we are children of light and the have defied being "CUT". At the DO's office the participants were encouraged to grow as good girls and praised them for their courageous decision.

After the address by the DO, the girls sang back to Kebabe Girls's Secondary school a kilometre away. Women and children from the neighbourhood joined the singing and marching to the centre. 441 Certificates of attendance and letters of appreciation were issued girl participants. The colourful ceremony ended with blessings and joint prayer.

Chapter Twelve
Conclusion

I liken a circumcised woman's body to a Toyota car engine with some of its essential parts have been stolen on transit. Gusii highlands have good amount of rain and farming soils. The road network is largely made of earth with many pot holes. Movement from one end to the other during rains is not easy. Fares hike and pushing and pulling the vehicles from the mud is a common site. Toyota cars have been noted to do excellent work in transporting passengers and goods. They are often seen on the neglected roads, overloaded with passengers and commercial goods. To continue doing the recommended hard job, the Toyota cars should have strong whole engines. Further, the clitoris in a woman body plays a major role intercourse and fulfillment. Without this essential part sexual relationship may be mechanical and only one-sided. This is depicted in "whole" uncircumcised woman. This is to say that circumcision for women is deplorable and uncalled for.

As the case of a Gusii woman like other African rural woman she does almost all pieces of odd jobs in the home, collecting firewood, water, feeding livestock, farm work apart from fulfilling her conjugal rights, reproduction and procreation. She therefore requires to be saved from the cruel knife of circumcision.

"Female circumcision is injurious to a woman's health," say many medical doctors I have spoken to. Abagusii need to appreciate that culture is not static and today we live in an ever changing, unpredictable and competitive world in which massive intellectual revolution is taking place. Our Abagusii society and individuals cannot afford to lag behind. Survival calls only for ensuring fitness and preparedness.

Certain risky human practices such as female circumcision must at some stage be abandoned in order to adopt a healthier and more helpful ones geared towards perpetuating life or the progeny while ensuring fulfilment of all in society. The speed with which these practices are discarded and/or new ones assimilated is very crucial. The factors influencing these changes are therefore crucial and also worth recognition. One such recognizable factor is the creation of awareness or highlighting of the problem. For without contrast or a reflecting surface there can be no image. No articles previously available have fairly, frankly and fearlessly expounded in depth the truth as it is with regard to Genital Mutilation. A vast majority of the Gusii tribesmen and by extension, most Kenyan communities are actually unaware of some self-destructive cultural and behavioural patterns that are rampant amongst them.

One impressive feature about this work is the provision of a solution or an alternative. The alternative, 'Rite of Passage' into womanhood without an actual 'cut' is recommended as so this practice has worked in some parts of Gusii. The Alternative Rite of Passage seminars which have been introduced by the church, gathers girls of circumcision age at a residential centre and teach the girls essential topics on how to enter womanhood without the cut, responsible adulthood, prominent and successful women of the bible and community, self-esteem, human anatomy and physiology and many more.

The author however cleverly realizes that the Female circumcision culture is deeply rooted and the Gusii society. This culture is a hard to die and the practice changes and is now done in secret by women medical practitioners. Gusii community is generally conservative and is impervious to change that the introduction to Alterative Rite of Passage is a temporary measure for now.

The Abagusii community like most African communities had its own fears based on superstitions and traditions. Female circumcision had and continues to contribute its own share of superstitions and fear. In his arguments the writer has rightly termed these superstitions and traditions as of no effect to human anatomy and physiology. Superstitions or traditions must not in any way dictate human procreation and productivity. Medically speaking as the writer points out, female Genital mutilation is injurious to a woman's physiological functions in both short and long time.

Transition from childhood to adulthood takes place in all females hailing from communities devoid of these rituals. Why not Gusii?

Chapter Thirteen: Appendices
Speeches at Kebabe Seminar

Speech by Ernest Munyi- District Commissioner, Nyamira District, during the opening ceremony of the Alternative Rite of Passage seminar at Kebabe Girls' Secondary school, on 29th November 1998.

The elimination female circumcision practice is a crucial goal that the community leaders need to address. I personally accepted to open this alternative rite of passage seminar since the practice is rampant in Nyamira District and thus requiring a consented effort. The significance of this initiation ceremony as a passage of rite for girls to adulthood has a positive societal cultural value. But the practice has serious consequences that outweigh its significance hence need to adopt a suitable alternative rite of passage.

Female circumcision is prevalent among several communities in Kenya that include the Meru's, Somali's, Kalenjins and Masai's. The boys also undergo circumcision in these communities as well as the Luhya community. The Luos initiation rituals involve removal of six lower teeth. These divergent cultural norms are continuously changing or replaced to fall witting conditions in the fast changing modern generation.

It should be noted that even in the biblical teachings only male circumcision is healthy and acceptable practice. On the other hand female circumcision there is known as female genital mutilation has had harmful effects that end up in deaths of the girl child. Some of the identified complications are bleeding, infections due to unhygienic conditions during operation, pains and psychological effects to the grandparents on consequences of the ritual are important.

The healthful personal is indicated to be involved in the FGM practice mainly for monetary gains. Emphasis to promote anti-FGM campaign among health personnel is crucial, as they are perceived to provide better services due to the risk of HIV/AIDS infection.

Alternative rite of passage is a newly introduced concept whose noble aim is to sensitize the communities that practice female circumcision into abandoning the practice and provide a suitable substitute to it. We fully support this concept wholeheartedly believing that in the near future this harmful practice will be history.

Female circumcision is commonly practiced in this district despite negative effects associated with it in almost all-traditional African societies, some form of rituals was performed to initiate youth into adulthood. For example among the Kikuyu men, Taita, Embu Kalenjin, Kisii, and Somali, circumcision of both boys and girls took place as a ritual of passage to adulthood. Other ethnic groups such as the Luhya only circumcised boys while the Luo had their front lower teeth removed.

There were also other traditional rituals performed like in the case of Masai who taught Moranism as a rite of passage into adult hood.

During circumcision girls were "taught" on how to become "women" while boys were taught on how to become "men". However, while male circumcision has been known and proven to be healthy and hygienic practices, female circumcision does not serve a purpose at all. It has been found to be harmful and automated. Indeed certain communities such as Kikuyu, Embu men, taita and Kalenjin have greatly reduced the number of girls that are circumcised. Others have abandoned it altogether and no longer practice it.

Circumcision of female has been established to be harmful practices that are why it is also known as female genital mutilation. Negative effects of female genital mutilation include:-

1. Excessive bleeding that may lead to anaemia and death.

2. Infection through use of unsterilized knives and treatment under unhygienic conditions because of secrecy associated with it. 3. Complications during child birth.

3. Transmission of STI and HIV/AIDS may take place as a result of using unsterilized and same knives on many girls.

These are also distortion of facts that go with female circumcision, that:-

1. Uncircumcised girl will never become a woman but will remain childish. This reasoning is absurd and has no basis at all.

2. Uncircumcised girl will never find a suitor.

The truth is that most men apart from the hypocrites prefer uncircumcised women. Any many uncircumcised women are married to men who come from communities who practice female circumcision.

There are certain trends to do with female genital mutilation that worries us:-

a) A lot of money is wasted during preparatory of girls to be circumcised. Money which could be invested in for school fees, books, school uniform in other words education and nutrition; balanced diet is spent on festivities associated with female circumcision. There should be no -pride at all in parents who spend thousands of shillings in circumcision ceremonies and get their daughter later attend school in term uniform or remain at home due to lack of school fees.

b) Another worrying trend is the involvement of health workers in this practice for commercial gains. Those health workers practising FGM not only exploit poor parents but also act unethically because they have become bush surgeons who operate in bushes and huts in secrecy in order to get a few hundred shillings to supplement their income. They earn a commission from peasant farmers to connect them to circumcisers. This unethical practice is abhorred and must stop.

FGM is also associated with ignorance and illiteracy. It is those still deeply entrenched in traditional belief systems and illiteracy that continue to practice FGM. hence all efforts should be made to educate girls in particular so that the practice dies a natural death. I emphasize girl education because those who strongly advocate for FGM are not men but women. It is mothers, aunties and grandmothers who don't want to let the practice to go. They want to cling on to it as long as they can because of distorted beliefs.

This problem therefore is not with young girls as such but with adamant adults, women. In fact it is these adults that we should be addressing today. However alternative rite of passage should be encouraged and even be made an annual event.

Lastly it is my prayer that all NGO's involved in the eradication of FGM in Nyamira district will present their programs and projects to our DDC so that their activities can be harmonized and coordinated for the good of the Abagusii of Nyamira district.

Thus there is need to integrate and coordinate the anti-FGM programs in the district with different stakeholders both private and public within the DDC institutional approach especially among non- governmental Organizations and ministry of health is to have a greater impact in developing appropriate intervention measures.

I take this opportunity to the SDA CHURCH and donor partners for facilitating this alternative rite of passage seminar. We cannot forget the parents of the 400 girls undergoing this ceremony for accepting not to perform the rituals on their daughters but avail them for education. I therefore declare the seminar officially opened.

Speech from the Medical Office of Health read on his behalf by David Gekara

Distinguished Guests, ladies and gentlemen: I do thank the organizers for promoting the anti-FGM campaign through this alternative rite of passage seminar. From the course outline a lot has been achieved by the girls in promoting their behaviour/growth in line with the cultural passage of rite. The ministry is concerned with the health of the girls especially in this particular era of the HIV/ AIDS pandemic as the FGM practice on serious health implications but seek to promote good moral values.

The fact that our medical personnel are involved in female circumcision in their own private capacity gives a negative image of the health workers. Despite the communities believe that it is safer to use the health personnel the ministry's is that it is medically unethical. An awareness creation on anti-FGM campaign is to be launched among the health personnel in the district to eliminate the practice.

I do request the seminar organizers to undertake an integrated approach to promote appropriate and acceptable alternative rite of passage curriculum. What has been achieved and recommend away forward for dissemination to the community members at grassroots level. The final report of the workshop is to provide a good basis for interventions and policy guidelines. Let us keep the fire rolling until elimination of female genital mutilation practice is complete.

Closing Speech from the Executive Director of SDA Church, Nyamira Conference - Pastor Richard Momanyi Nyakego

What is Education?

The darkness if far gone — Ephesians 5:8

You are a peculiar people — 1 Peter 2:9-10

When you have got the light you have no excuse again to walk in the darkness. You should walk in the light. In the light of the knowledge which you have secured in the seminar *Alternative Rite of Passage* I hope you will be the light bearers to wherever you will go.

When we talk of culture, tradition, behaviour I believe that these things are dynamic, they keep change from time to time. The way we live today is not the way our grandparents lived. They used to pit on skins of animals. Why are we not there if we live going to culture? There was no formal education as we have it today. We have been civilized that is what we say.

This has been a gradual, not the whole thing at the same time; this has affected our way of eating, dressing, behaviour and worship. So, when we talk of change we have to admit of change. The perception of this change is what the issue now.

Coming to the issue at hand, that is FGM, allow me to call it "female cut". We look back to basis. It is rightly stated in the Bible the instructions given by God to Abraham, him and his family male- were to be circumcised -this is not the case with his wife, if it was, then God could have specified- Genesis 17:10 the origin of this act then is with the culture, which we have found that culture is dynamic.

Its purpose:-

The "cutting" of the flesh was a symbol of leaving the period of childhood to pave way to adulthood, which was full of responsibility at home and in the tribe. At the same time it was a gate to marriage.

Today duties and responsibilities are better evaluated in the background of academic and educational prosperity; economic success contribution to national development and cultural evaluation that should involve change of practice from what is not beneficial to that, which is. Does this cut affect marriage?

In those days the days if our grandparents those who were initiated were taught how to live harmoniously with the young, their age mates, old people and members of the opposite sex. They were given instructions about life of the people, their history, traditions and beliefs and above all how to raise a family. The "female cut" was a "certificate" for a girl to get married and have children. Therefore many rituals and secrets instilled to the ones who were undergoing this process.

Nowadays with the rapid changes taking place in the world, we should understand and even read signs of the times. Let's not display our ignorance. The truth of the matter is let's shun the habit. The government should continue to fight and give maximum support, as the church is doing her part in the eradication of FGM- which has no educational, social, physical or moral value at the moment.

In a very special way I would like to thank the following Anti-FGM facilitators who have made this occasion a success:

Daniel M. Mokaya - Project coordinator

Johnson Masimba - Nurse/facilitator

Pauline Mogeni - Nurse/facilitator

David Omare - Administrator/ facilitator

The church pastors, donors, Ministry of Health, the provincial administration and all that have laid a hand in this good cause.

Let us fight together for the elimination of this female circumcision practice.

Appendix A
Kisii Proverbs Used in the Book & Their meaning

1. *Ensinyo nekona gosaka mabe na maya*
   - the border is expected to produce bad or good news of war and peace

2. *Ensinyo manakobengwa mbamura etabwati*
   - when people retreat and backup from the common border it is an indication that there no brave men from defence

3. *Bange mbaya korende mbariete kiane nkaigwa bobe*
   If you want work done in time you need many people, but the only disadvantage is that they eat much not like one person may eat.

4. *Getiro kemogondo 'moserengeti ore eero*
   - it is a easier to join the drinking party than the one working or doing manual labour in the fields.

5. *Rioba nderere nainche nkorere*
   - a new mother requests the power of the sun to bless her newly born baby while she takes great care on same the baby. Kisii prayer.

6. *Ekiomogoko nomwana ogetoire*
   - selfish persons have no choice to provide food when a daughter or son is being circumcision or has been born. Through children there is a blessing of getting more food in such occasion.

7. *Tinkweba ase rorera na ase getinge*
   - a woman is likely not to forget where she was born and where she is married to.

8. *Omosacha iroka*
   – a man's fertility is lifetime.

9. *Bogundo mbwanyene ke eamate echana bosa igo*
   - When a family members dies, close relatives takes a burden but the neighbours mourn for a short while and leave to do their business as usual.

10. *Nchogu ya mete menge*
    – *Nchogu ya mete menge* – an elephant eats different plants and so is a disease to be treated by many drugs or medicines before there is certainty of a patient getting well.

11. *Makoro magoti nande achicha*
    – Culture is dynamic; it keeps changing.

12. *Echae yamorero*
    - Literary used as hot tea given to women who accompany a girl for circumcision in the morning

For a comprehensive list of Abagusii proverbs refer to Nemwel Atemba's *Abagusii Wisdom Revisited*, Nsemia Inc. Publishers, 2010.

Appendix B
Glossary of Terms

Abagusii - Bantu people in   Kenya living in Gusii highlands

Amabuko -A plat with a sweet smell used to make a cage like structure for the circumcised boy or girl.

Amarwa - Locally made beer made from finger-millet, *obori, maize or some other cereal.*

Chibarongo - Human twins. Animal twins are known as *chisare*

Chinyangi - Rituals and rites performed to the circumcised. They are performed by only those who have undergone the same rituals. This is an important period for instruction ad teaching the circumcised boy or girl.

Chisosokoro - Ancestors

Ebibasane -   Circumcised girls before they heal the cut wound.

Ebundo - A kid of red earth mixed with water to make a mixture to smear on the face of the circumcised boy or girl before graduating to adulthood.

Egesagane - Uncircumcised girl or woman

Egesanda - A vessel for drinking water or beer. It is made from the calabash by cutting it into two halves from top to bottom.

Egesangio - a group of persons working for each other in turns.

Egesiringi - A kind of plant that is used to make arrows.

Egetinti - A ring made of beads of many beautiful colours usually worn by circumcised girls during the last ceremony before she is declared *omoiseke*. A circumcised and successful graduate of *obware*.

Egetonto - A bamboo type of plant

Egetoro - Donation in cash or in kind.

Egwagwa - A climbing plant worn by women as camouflage while dancing

Ekee - A large basket made from reeds for serving ugali made from reeds of finger millet.

Ekegenga - Apiece of burning wood

Ekegusii - a language of Abagusii people in Kenya

Ekeiririato - A loud shout of happiness applause or cheer, ululation.

Ekemoya - a small skin sew bag where the circumcision knife is kept

Ekemunu - A smaller basket(see ekee) used for carrying flour and used for drinking beer.

Ekerandi - A kind of calabash used for storage of sour milk or porridge.

Ekerundu - A type of plant that is carried by boys and girls after circumcision. It is taboo for the circumcised to loose it during the time of seclusion.

Ekieyo - A type of hard wood that has good charcoal. It is used to keep the ritual fire burning.

E*murwa* - a kind of fast growing grass found where cows live (*boma*)

Eng'iti - A game performed to test the bravery of the circumcised boy or girl. The apparatus makes a deep scary sound. When it is played in the dark, it is even more scary.

Engori - A rope made from sisal fibers

Enkuuri - A term used to refer to the boys or girls who scream or cry while they are being circumcised. Usually they are despised ad are said to bring shame to the family.

Enyabubu - A flat wood measuring about five inches tied to a string. It makes noise when it is repeatedly swung over the shoulders.

Esaro - A small leather bag for keeping money, knives or finger millet.

Esasi - Dry leaves of 'omosabakwa' tree or dry cow dung that is used to start sparks of fire after friction.

Esimbore - A circumcision song
Esubo - A second ritual for circumcised girls. When used as a verb it means torture. *Esuguta* - A small bush that grows in marshy areas. It is planted and watered in the house by the circumcised boys and girls.

Eyarogoro - A song sang during the graduation morning of the circumcised girls.

Obori - Finger millet, whose flour is used to cook ugali or make porridge common in Gusii highlands. Most women from Gusii are said to be fertile because of this.

Obware - circumcision, the rite of passage from childhood to adulthood

Obweri/ bweri - A cowshed or living area for cattle

Ogochoba - The art of me stealthily entering a house where girls are performing rituals for the purpose of having sexual intercourse.

Ogokoma - a act or game of seeing another circumcised boy or girl first so as to become a winner.

Ogokonga - See *ogokoma*

Omobera - A good hard wood tree that makes good charcoal for the ritual fire.

Omoiseke - A girl or woman that is circumcised and has successfully undergone all rites and rituals.

Omoisia - Uncicumcised boy or man.

Omokebi - also known as omosari, a woman or man who circumcises

Omokorogoinywa - A tree that produces wild edible fruits which ca be used to kindle the ritual fire.

Omomura - A circumcised boy or man who has undergone all rituals and rites

Omonyenya - A hard wood used to kindle the ritual fire.

Omoraa - A hardwood that is used for kindling the ritual fire.

Omosabakwa - A kid of tree that is used to kindle the ritual fire. Its dry leaves are also used for starting the sparks of the fire from the friction *'ogosegesa'*. The tree is also used as a female part during the making of fire by friction. At times boys are circumcised under this kind of tree.

Omosari - see *omokebi*

Omosegi - An instructor or teacher for the circumcised boy or girl during the seclusion period. He or she should have undergone successfully the rites and rituals of circumcision.

Omosocho - A sacred tree under which boys are circumcised.. Its wood is used to make sacrificial wooden cups and bowls.

Omosogwa - A thorny tree.

Omotobo - A kind of plant that produces wild fruits resembling lemons. Its ash is used to cure tobacco. It is also used in making a yoke for oxen and also good for kindling the ritual fire.

Omware - A circumcised girl or boy during the period of seclusion.

Orogio - A piece of broke pot

Riburu - A small cage-like structure made of *amabuko* used by the circumcised girl or boy during the period of seclusion.

Rinagu -A kind of green vegetable that has a bitter taste. It is very commonly eaten by   Abagusii

Risaga - a group of people invited to work in exchange for food or beer.

Ritierio - a whetstone

Saiga - A small hut I which men lived or where the circumcised boys stayed during the time of seclusion.

Appendix C
Names of Plants & Trees Used in the Book

	Vernacular name	Scientific name	Page
1	*Amabuko*	uknown	47, 50, 106,
2	*Chinsaga (Orosaga)*	Gynandropsis gynandra (syn. Cleome gynandra)	39,
3	*Egesiringi*	unknown	106,
4	*Egetonto*	Euphorbia ingens (Candelabra tree)	106,
5	*Egwagwa*	Mormodica foetica	106,
6	*Ekerandi*	Curcubitaceae (Lagenaria sphaerica)	107,
7	*Ekerundu*	Sida cordifolia	107,
8	*Ekieyo*	unknown	107, 30,
9	*Emurwa*	Pennisetum clandestimum	51, 107,
10	*Entamame*	Crassocephalum vitellinum	35,
11	*Esuguta*	Pennisetum schimberi	50, 107, 44, 45, 47
12	*Obori*	Eleusine corocan	108, 30,
13	*Omobera*	unknown	108,30,
14	*Omokonge*	Acacia gerraldi	30
15	*Omokorogoinwa*	Dovyalis kafra	108,
16	*Omonyenya*	Acacia nilotica	108,30,
17	*Omoraa*	Olea Africana	108,30,
18	*Omosabakwa*	Vernonia auriculifera	107, 108, 30
19	*Omosocho*	Croton macrostachyus	109,
20	*Omosogwa*	Dovyalis macrocalyx	109,
21	*Omotamaywa*	unkown	30,
22	*Omotandege*	Acacia mearnsii (Black wattle)	30,
23	*Omotobo*	unkown	109,
24	*Omwobo*	Markhamia lutea	30,
25	*Rinagu*	Solanum nigrum	109, 39

Source: E.G. Nyarangi, *Some Plants of Gusii* ,2011. Unpublished manuscript).

Appendix D
Bibliography

- "Daily Nation" a daily newspaper - various articles.
- "Kenya times" a daily newspaper - various articles.
- Catholic Church, *Pastoral letter of the Bishops of Kenya, December 1999.*
- *Convention on the rights of the child-* adopted by the General Assembly of the United Nations on 20th November 1989
- *Equality Now*, a magazine from the international Human rights organization that works to end violence and discrimination against women.
- J.S. Mbiti, *African Religions and Philosophy.*
- Jomo Kenyatta, *Facing Mount Kenya*, (tribal life of the Gikuyu)
- Ministry of Planning and National Development, *Kisii, Development plan 1989-1993*
- Office of the Vice President and Ministry of Planning and National Development *Nyamira District Development Plan 1997-2001*
- Maendeleo ya wanawake Organization - A women organization in Kenya
- Nahid Toubia, *Female Genital Mutilation*, A call for Action, Rainbow New York
- Nelson King'oina Nyang'era, *The making of man and woman under Abagusii Customary Laws.*
- Ngugi wa Thing'o, *The River Between*
- Nyaundi N., *Seventh Day Adventism in Gusii, Kenya*
- Primary Source- interviews on Female Genital Mutilation.
- Program of Appropriate Technology in Health (PATH) Kenya
- Seventh Day Adventist Church - *General Conference) Statements, Guidelines and other documents*
- Seventh day Adventist Church, *Reports and Minutes*
- *William Robert Ochieng, Pre-colonial History of Gusii of Western Kenya (1974)*